B

WILLIAM SHAKESPEARE'S

A Midsummer Night's Dream

BARRON'S BOOK NOTES

WILLIAM SHAKESPEARE'S

A Midsummer Night's Dream

BY

George Loutro

SERIES COORDINATOR

Murray Bromberg
Principal, Wang High School of Queens
Holliswood, New York

Past President
High School Principals Association of New York City

BARRON'S EDUCATIONAL SERIES, INC.
New York • London • Toronto • Sydney

ACKNOWLEDGMENTS

Our thanks to Milton Katz and Julius Liebb for their contribution to the *Book Notes* series.

Loreto Todd, Senior Lecturer in English, University of Leeds, England, prepared the chapter on Elizabethan English in this book.

All inquiries should be addressed to:
Barron's Educational Series, Inc.
250 Wireless Boulevard
Hauppauge, New York 11788

Library of Congress Catalog Card No. 85-39/2

International Standard Book No. 0-8120-3527-5

Library of Congress Cataloging in Publication Data

— — — — — — — —

   William Shakespeare's A midsummer night's dream.

   (Barron's book notes)
   Bibliography: p. 124
   Summary: A guide to reading "A Midsummer Night's
Dream" with a critical and appreciative mind. Includes
background on the author's life and times, sample tests,
term paper suggestions, and a reading list.
   1. Shakespeare, William, 1564–1616. Midsummer
night's dream. [1. Shakespeare, William, 1564–1616.
Midsummer night's dream. 2. English literature—
History and criticism] I. Title. II. Series.
PR2827.S38 1985   822.3'3   85-3972
ISBN 0-8120-3527-5

PRINTED IN THE UNITED STATES OF AMERICA

123   550   98765432

CONTENTS

Advisory Board   vii
How to Use This Book   ix
THE AUTHOR AND HIS TIMES   1
THE PLAY   8
The Plot   8
The Characters   11
Other Elements   22
      Setting   22
      Themes   23
      Style   27
      Elizabethan English 29
      Point of View 35
      Form and Structure 36
      Sources   37
      The Globe Theatre 40
The Play   45
A STEP BEYOND   111
Tests and Answers   111
Term Paper Ideas and other Topics
  for Writing   122
Further Reading   124
      Critical Works 124
      Author's Works 125
The Critics   127

ADVISORY BOARD

We wish to thank the following educators who helped us focus our *Book Notes* series to meet student needs and critiqued our manuscripts to provide quality materials.

Sandra Dunn, English Teacher
Hempstead High School, Hempstead, New York

Lawrence J. Epstein, Associate Professor of English
Suffolk County Community College, Selden, New York

Leonard Gardner, Lecturer, English Department
State University of New York at Stony Brook

Beverly A. Haley, Member, Advisory Committee
National Council of Teachers of English Student
Guide Series, Fort Morgan, Colorado

Elaine C. Johnson, English Teacher
Tamalpais Union High School District
Mill Valley, California

Marvin J. LaHood, Professor of English
State University of New York College at Buffalo

Robert Lecker, Associate Professor of English
McGill University, Montréal, Québec, Canada

David E. Manly, Professor of Educational Studies
State University of New York College at Geneseo

Bruce Miller, Associate Professor of Education
State University of New York at Buffalo

Frank O'Hare, Professor of English and
Director of Writing
Ohio State University, Columbus, Ohio

Faith Z. Schullstrom, Member, Executive Committee
National Council of Teachers of English
Director of Curriculum and Instruction
Guilderland Central School District, New York

Mattie C. Williams, Director, Bureau of Language Arts
Chicago Public Schools, Chicago, Illinois

HOW TO USE THIS BOOK

You have to know how to approach literature in order to get the most out of it. This *Barron's Book Notes* volume follows a plan based on methods used by some of the best students to read a work of literature.

Begin with the guide's section on the author's life and times. As you read, try to form a clear picture of the author's personality, circumstances, and motives for writing the work. This background usually will make it easier for you to hear the author's tone of voice, and follow where the author is heading.

Then go over the rest of the introductory material—such sections as those on the plot, characters, setting, themes, and style of the work. Underline, or write down in your notebook, particular things to watch for, such as contrasts between characters and repeated literary devices. At this point, you may want to develop a system of symbols to use in marking your text as you read. (Of course, you should only mark up a book you own, not one that belongs to another person or a school.) Perhaps you will want to use a different letter for each character's name, a different number for each major theme of the book, a different color for each important symbol or literary device. Be prepared to mark up the pages of your book as you read. Put your marks in the margins so you can find them again easily.

Now comes the moment you've been waiting for—the time to start reading the work of literature. You may want to put aside your *Barron's Book Notes* volume until you've read the work all the way through. Or you may want to alternate, reading the *Book Notes* analysis of each section as soon as you have finished reading the corresponding part of the original. Before you move on, reread crucial passages you don't fully understand. (Don't take this guide's analysis for granted—make up your own mind as to what the work means.)

Once you've finished the whole work of literature, you may want to review it right away, so you can firm up your ideas about what it means. You may want to leaf through the book concentrating on passages you marked in reference to one character or one theme. This is also a good time to reread the *Book Notes* introductory material, which pulls together insights on specific topics.

When it comes time to prepare for a test or to write a paper, you'll already have formed ideas about the work. You'll be able to go back through it, refreshing your memory as to the author's exact words and perspective, so that you can support your opinions with evidence drawn straight from the work. Patterns will emerge, and ideas will fall into place; your essay question or term paper will almost write itself. Give yourself a dry run with one of the sample tests in the guide. These tests present both multiple-choice and essay questions. An accompanying section gives answers to the multiple-choice questions as well as suggestions for writing the essays. If you have to select a term paper topic, you may choose one from the list of suggestions in this book. This guide also provides you with a reading list, to help you when you start research for a term paper, and a selection of provocative comments by critics, to spark your thinking before you write.

THE AUTHOR AND HIS TIMES

As we might expect from the range and vitality of Shakespeare's writing, Elizabethan England was an exciting and changing place. Though we know little of Shakespeare's own life, we know much about his world. For England, the sixteenth century was a period of growth and exploration, contributing to a renaissance in cultural and economic life. Under the reigns of Elizabeth I (1558–1603) and James I (1603–1625), London became one of the artistic and mercantile centers of Europe. We can still see the beauty of its half-timbered houses, its bridge-towers and churches. But above all, the literature of the period continues to excite the minds of readers, offering great riches of imagination and language.

For Shakespeare and his contemporaries, the English language was changing and growing. Dictionaries had not yet solidified spelling and meaning, and sometimes Elizabethan poetry seems to be possessed of a great unrefined power. Poets and playwrights—among them Edmund Spenser, Ben Jonson, Christopher Marlowe, as well as Shakespeare—reveled in the riches of this emerging language and created a brilliant new drama.

It is well to remember that in Shakespeare's time theater was a popular pastime (something like movies are today), attended by both commonfolk and royalty. It was not merely the province of an intellectual few. Folk traditions of ballad and song, as well as the Christian miracle and mystery plays, had accustomed the people to poetic drama, its speeches cast in rhyme and meter. And the Elizabethan theater highlighted the spoken word. It used few stage properties and almost no scenery. Its outdoor circular theaters surrounded a bare apron-shaped stage. The characters came and left at a fast pace, and what they *said* indicated who and where they were. The Elizabethan audience was attentive to the spoken word. A playwright might as easily present his ideas and actions in the form of poetic images or narrative speeches, for the theater was a place in which the ear, not merely the eye, was dazzled. And this was the kind of environment especially well suited for William Shakespeare.

You will see in *A Midsummer Night's Dream* how appropriate this poetic method is. The fairy world comes alive not from stage tricks, elaborate costumes, and airy sets, but through poetry. Detailed fantastic descriptions, cascades of named flowers, images of a powerful and mysterious natural world—these are what make the fairy world vivid. The magic lives in Shakespeare's language.

The world of his writing is filled with cultural riches, extraordinary characters, and historical events. But of Shakespeare's own life we know little. He was born in the small town of Stratford in 1564, around the 23rd of April. His baptism certificate tells us that. His father was a somewhat well-to-do merchant and councilman whose fortunes seemed to slip as Shakespeare grew older. In all probability he saw to it that William took advantage of the public education available to all the sons of Stratford's citizens. But most of what we know about Shakespeare in this early period is conjecture. The only other certain information we have is his marriage, in 1582, to Ann Hathaway, a woman eight years older than he. Since a child Susanna was born six months later, the bride was already pregnant at the time of the wedding. In 1585, the twins Hamnet and Judith were born.

For the rest—at least regarding Stratford—there is only legend. Some say Shakespeare was booted out of town for poaching at a neighboring estate; others say he taught school. We do know that around 1587 Shakespeare left Stratford for the creative opportunity to be found in the big city of London. Its lure would be the same as that of any metropolis today: a rich and varied cultural life, political power-broking, history in the making, pageantry, and the good life. Perhaps he apprenticed himself to one of the local theater companies right away. But in truth we don't know how he became such an accomplished writer so quickly. By 1592 he was already being attacked by a local playwright, Robert Greene, for being an "upstart crowe," an actor who would be better off leaving the writing of plays to real playwrights. The furor that followed this famous accusation shows that Shakespeare had established a considerable reputation by the time it was written. No one bothers to attack an unknown writer. And the accusation, importantly, also reminds us that Shakespeare was an actor as well as a writer. All his life he combined these two vocations, giving him special entry into the world of theater, its nuances, and the interplay between the acted and written word. By 1593 he'd also proved himself a commanding poet with the publication of the poem *Venus and Adonis*, followed the next year by *The Rape of Lucrece*.

For the next eighteen or twenty years Shakespeare produced a succession of plays that mark him as the premier poet and playwright of his age— perhaps the finest the English language has seen. Through comedies, histories, and tragedies he speaks of his time and world with an authority that makes them seem, generation after generation, completely contemporary. He was fortunate to have a company of actors throughout his writing life with which he could work, gaining from the traded insights and from the ability of seeing his work produced. He was able to benefit from the resources of the finest Elizabethan outdoor playhouse, the Globe, so that his work had a state-of-the-art theater in which to be performed. He had noble patronage to help him at the beginning (the Earl of Southampton) and even royal favor when his patron became embroiled in an unsuccessful coup d'état and was imprisoned. Instead of trouble, Shakespeare found grace: by the time James I assumed the throne in 1603, Shakespeare's players, formerly associated as the Chamberlain's Men, were now called the King's Men, receiving royal patronage and favor.

Around 1611 Shakespeare retired from London and the theater, to return to his family at Stratford. He presumably lived out his life peacefully, dying in 1616. But once again legend obscures fact. A famous tombstone inscription, ascribed to him, seeks to gain him a peaceful death as well; it reads, "Blest be the man that spares these stones,/And curst be he that moves my bones." No one has moved them.

Shakespeare was unique among the world's great dramatists in his ability to create the finest examples of both comedy and tragedy. That the same writer could produce both *King Lear* and *A Midsummer Night's Dream*, *Hamlet* and *The Tempest*, has been a source of wonderment to millions of readers. Also, his complex English-history plays, with their multiple plots and points of view, have influenced the way we think of history itself. The wide range of Shakespeare's achievement was boldly set forth in the first edition of his complete dramatic works in 1623 when the publishers divided what has come to be known as the "First Folio" into Comedies, Histories, and Tragedies.

Despite this variety, there are ways in which *King Lear* could only have been written by the author of *A Midsummer Night's Dream*. One way is that in both plays no character's perspective is sufficient to judge everyone else's. Also, merely understanding a human problem will not solve it without a transformation of another sort, a genuine change of heart. And throughout his comedies, this most witty writer kept vivid the sense that wit alone is not an adequate response to people and situations.

An early comedy, almost overflowing with witty wordplay, is *Love's Labour's Lost*. The lesson learned by its principal characters is that words and wit must be tempered by concern for others' feelings. And as with most of his comedies, part of the play is set in a special place where transformations can take place more freely, outside the busy world of court or city. In *A Midsummer Night's Dream*, the lovers expend great energy speaking in witty romantic repartee. And the fairies' forest is the magical place that surrounds their transformations. In *The Merchant of Venice*, another early comedy, Belmont, where Portia lives, is the special place; in *As You Like It* it is the forest of Arden.

In the so-called "dark" comedies (*All's Well That*

Ends Well, Troilus and Cressida, Measure for Measure) the magic place where people can be revealed and healed almost disappears. Lechery, spitefulness, and selfishness are exposed rather than transformed. But in the later comedies, sometimes called the "romances," healing magic returns: *Pericles, Cymbeline, The Winter's Tale,* and *The Tempest.* In fact, the whole of *The Tempest* takes place on a magic island ruled by a sorcerer who has the knowledge and power to transform the rational forces that had exiled him years before. Prospero is a wiser, more mature Oberon, and his attendant Ariel is a more spiritual Puck.

A Midsummer Night's Dream was probably written around 1594. Some scholars suggest it was written to be performed at a noble wedding ceremony, perhaps that of William Stanley, Earl of Denby, to Elizabeth Vere in 1595. This is pure speculation, however, fueled by the importance of marriage to the play. Its similarity in language and theme to *Romeo and Juliet* also helps date the play. Though one is a comedy and the other a tragedy, both deal with the nature of love, its impulsive judgments and vows. Romeo and Juliet are tricked by their fate, ending in death. But fate, in the form of Oberon, interferes on behalf of the lovers in *A Midsummer Night's Dream*, and their trials end in marriage.

Though it comes early in Shakespeare's career, *A Midsummer Night's Dream* shows his command of the different strands that combined to make great Elizabethan drama. In his courtly subplot of Theseus and Hippolyta, Shakespeare demonstrates his familiarity with classical subjects. He interweaves mythic and historical material to give his characters an imposing royal stature. With the lovers, Shakespeare shows his command of romantic poetry, the formal language of love developed centuries earlier by the troubadors of France. Though he is mocking in tone with the lovers, he gives romantic poetry a free reign with Oberon and Titania, who draw on folk ballads and pastoral traditions to create the magic of high poetry. And with Bottom and his rustic comrades, Shakespeare develops a realism based on Christian folk plays that enables him to bring all kinds and classes of people into his art. *A Midsummer Night's Dream* offers a unique blending of styles, characters, and realms of experience into a unified work of art.

Shakespeare's life in London was filled with a similar mix of people and types. It was a throbbing metropolis for its time, bursting the bounds of its medieval walls. But its modernity was tempered by the folk traditions and beliefs of the people who streamed to its streets. In the life of the English countryside the mythic, legendary fairies and elves—known from centuries of ancient Celtic traditions—still had a place. Shakespeare was able to combine this magic imaginary world with the contemporary urban landscape of London. Watch the ways in which he is able to include all kinds of people, and different dimensions of experience, to paint a picture that in the largest possible sense parallels the world in which he lived.

THE PLAY

The Plot

In the ancient city of Athens a wedding is about to take place between Theseus, duke of Athens, and Hippolyta, the Amazon warrior queen whom he has wooed and won. They meet in the duke's palace to discuss their marriage festivities. Suddenly, Egeus storms in, extremely upset. He wants his daughter, Hermia, to marry Demetrius, who is dutifully in love with her. Hermia, however, is in love with Lysander and refuses to give in to her father's demands. The two suitors and the woman they both love state their case before the duke. Theseus explains that Athenian law is on the side of the father: Hermia must heed his wishes, not follow her own desire. In fact, Hermia must either obey the law, remain a virgin and enter a nunnery, or die! Hermia is given until the next new moon—the wedding day of Theseus and Hippolyta—to make her decision. She and Lysander secretly plan, instead, to flee Athens and live outside of town with an aunt of Lysander's. Another young woman, Helena, arrives. She is in love with Demetrius, but he will have none of her. The lovers tell her of their plan to elope.

In the house of Quince, a carpenter, several Athenian workingmen meet to discuss their plans to present a play as entertainment for the wedding of the duke. Quince, Snug, Bottom, Flute, Snout, and Starveling have decided on a play entitled "The most lamentable comedy, and most cruel death of

Pyramus and Thisby." Parts are assigned to each player, but only after Bottom, full of boundless energy and enthusiasm, shows how he could play all the parts himself. They agree to rehearse the following evening in a wood outside of town.

The scene shifts to that Athenian wood, but now the players are of an entirely different order. They are Oberon, the king of the fairies, his queen, Titania, and Puck (or Robin Goodfellow), a spritely attendant of the king. Oberon and Titania have been quarreling over the possession of a young Indian boy that both want, but the Queen will not hand him over. Oberon, with the aid of Puck, plans his revenge on Titania. He will drop the juice of a magic flower into the eyes of his sleeping queen. When she awakes, she will fall in love with whomever (or whatever) she sees first, preferably "some vile thing." Then she will forget about the boy!

Meanwhile, Demetrius and Helena enter the wood. Seeing Helena's loveless plight, Oberon instructs Puck to charm the eyes of Demetrius as well, so that he will love Helena.

Now Lysander and Hermia arrive, en route to their elopement. Mistaking Lysander for Demetrius, Puck anoints the eyes of Lysander, who awakes and declares his love for Helena. Hermia awakes in the woods alone, having dreamt of a serpent eating her heart.

On time for their rehearsal, the workingmen also arrive in the wood and begin to sort out "Pyramus and Thisby." Mischievous Puck jumps at the chance to cause trouble. He catches Bottom and places an ass's head on him. The other rustics flee in terror. But Titania's reaction is different. Charmed by the love juice, she immediately falls in love with Bottom, ass's head and all.

The lovers regroup in confusion. Now both Lysander and Demetrius profess love for Helena instead of for Hermia. Angers flare up and swords are drawn, but Puck leads everyone in magic circles so no real harm comes. Oberon, seeing the mistake that has taken place, has Puck remove the charm from Lysander's eyes so that his love returns for Hermia. Demetrius remains "enchanted" with his Helena.

Titania is also released from her enchantment. Reunited with Oberon, she surrenders the Indian boy to the king. The lovers, startled by the arrival of Theseus and his court, awaken as if from a mysterious dream, properly in love with each other, but startled as to how they've gotten there. Theseus, finding that things have worked out rather neatly, overrides Egeus and announces that the three weddings will take place simultaneously. Bottom is relieved of his ass's head and returns to Quince's house to continue rehearsing the play.

In the palace of Theseus, preparations commence for the wedding festivities. Bottom and company perform their "lamentable comedy." A comedy it is, and though the duke and the others offer much jesting commentary about the production, they are ultimately well pleased with the entertainment. The three sets of newlyweds adjourn to their beds.

Puck arrives to sweep away the last grains of sleepy enchantment. Oberon and Titania offer blessings upon the houses of the lovers. Puck, with a glint in his eye, asks for applause. After all, he suggests, these proceedings may have been nothing "but a dream."

The Characters

Theseus

As duke of Athens, Theseus occupies an important social and political position that is at the heart of his character. Though he had a lively past, filled with heroic war exploits and romantic conquests, he now is a figure of the Athenian establishment, upholding the social order. As such, he represents, in contrast to the volatile lovers, the stabilizing force of marriage.

Theseus is a traditional Greek mythic hero. He is mentioned in many ancient texts, including Homer, Euripides, Plutarch, and Ovid. He is probably most famous for having killed the monstrous Minotaur, in the labyrinth of Minos on Crete. Though there is occasional mention of his former deeds, the person of Shakespeare's Theseus is as much the playwright's invention as he is a legendary figure.

With his upholding of the social order comes Theseus's praise of reason as a primary power. He and Hippolyta are untouched by the fairy realm. They seem to be above the magic, but you might also see them as being outside of it. Theseus's reliance on reason blocks him off from some of the more mystical realms of human experience. In Act V, he draws a famous comparison between the lover, the lunatic, and the poet. He feels they are all under the sway of their imaginations, which blinds them to reality. In consequence, some realms of passion and art are closed to him.

Theseus may be trapped in his position, or he may be filling it grandly. In either case, he has a kindly awareness of his subjects. Though he may not be appreciative of art per se, he understands the good intentions of the actors. He knows that his position alone has a certain power and seeks to use it with a clear and just mind.

Hippolyta

A warrior in her own right, Hippolyta maintains a kind of aloof dignity. She too is a Greek legendary figure, an Amazon queen of fierce pride and strength. In the beginning of the play she counters Theseus's impatience for the wedding day with a cool, imperial rationality of her own. Yet she doesn't rely so completely on reason: she is charmed and a little disturbed by the lovers' stories. She's not willing to discount their tales completely. While viewing the performance of the rustic workingmen, she seems to be impatient with the amateur nature of the production, though she warms to it by the end. Perhaps she too feels the necessity to temper her natural passions with a stateliness proper to her office. Compare her to the emotionally stormy lovers. How might her reserve be seen as a more mature kind of relating? Both she and Theseus bracket the play, beginning and end, like the pillars of society between which the Midsummer Madness occurs.

Hermia

Hermia shows her spunkiness right from the beginning. Though the force of familial and social power are brought heavily to bear upon her, she sticks to her guns. Her first words are a defense of Lysander against the accusations of her father, Egeus, and Theseus. She asks that her father look with her eyes, to try to see her viewpoint. She stands up for what she believes in even though it may mean her death. It's easy to side with Hermia—but what could you say in defense of her father's position?

Hermia is unswerving in her devotion to Lysander through all his changes and always gives him the benefit of the doubt. She loves him with an authenticity that goes beyond "doting," and her pain at being betrayed by him seems equally real.

She is described as having a dark complexion and being small, but you don't get more physical detail than that. Her temper is as fierce as her love; when it's kindled by jealousy toward Helena, she turns into a real spitfire. Although, especially in the beginning, Hermia speaks the proper courtly romantic poetry with Lysander, she shows that there is something beyond propriety in her character. But when it comes to defending her virgin modesty in the woods, she's quick to make Lysander keep his distance.

Hermia's combination of passion and judgment is set off from the feelings of all the other lovers. She knows what she wants, is willing to make great sacrifices for it, will fight like a lioness in defense of it, and ultimately trusts in her power. She's not above love-foolishness, but she gives to the romantic comedy a sturdy foundation.

Lysander
It's hard to get a grip on the character of Lysander. Indeed, because of the frustrating interference of

Puck, it's hard for him to keep a grip on himself. As you read the play, you may have difficulty telling him and Demetrius apart. They both seem to be defined more by the object of their desires than by any qualities in and of themselves.

Lysander has the unlucky distinction of professing his undying eternal love for two different women, one after the other. It certainly makes us suspicious of the steadfastness of his character. Consequently, the beautiful, flowery, romantic poetry he speaks rings hollow. He's made the butt of Shakespeare's ironic comedy of fickle love. He goes through all the right motions, says all the right words, but doesn't show any depth of character. He defends his new infatuation with Helena by swearing it comes from reason. But since you know it comes from Cupid's magic flower, both Lysander's love and reason seem suspect. His normalcy is his main characteristic: he's just a lover, doing the foolish things that lovers do. Therefore, don't be too hard on him. Look at him through Hermia's eyes; why do you think she loves him? We see many ways in which his love seems false, but in what ways do you view his love as true?

Helena

Helena is primarily defined by her relationship to love, but unfortunately that love is lacking. The unhappy experience of unrequited love seems to have penetrated to her very core. Although attractive, tall, and willowy, she questions her own virtues because being unloved makes her feel unworthy of love.

It's true that Demetrius originally loved her, and she has cause for being upset that he now seems to care for Hermia. But Helena is a prime example of the ill effects of "doting" too much: she loses respect for herself and, consequently, some of ours for her. Her running after Demetrius seems foolish and shallow to many readers. Do you think she is a prime target for some feminist consciousness-raising? She's throwing herself away for a man you have reason to believe isn't all that worthy.

Helena is so used to being rejected that she might not be able to recognize real love if it came her way. When both Lysander and Demetrius turn their loving gazes on her, she can only suspect that they're making fun of her. Though you know she's right to doubt their sincerity, what would have happened if one of them were sincere? Even at the end, she feels that Demetrius is hers, and yet somehow is not. Since he's the one holdover with charmed eyes, she's more correct than she knows. Neither she nor Hermia speaks in the last act. Perhaps they're both wondering about what they've gotten, having gotten what they supposedly wanted.

Demetrius

Like Lysander, Demetrius is difficult to identify except by his relation to the one he loves, or, more particularly, to the one who loves him. Helena's chasing after him and his irritation with her are the primary marks of his character. Since in his uncharmed state he even threatens Helena with bodily harm, he comes off as not quite the gracious courtly lover he means to be. And you may wonder, too, about how easily his eye was distracted from Helena by Hermia in the first place. His constant remarks at the performance of "Pyramus and

Thisby" show him to be clever, but maybe a little rude, too. In any event, as the one person still under the spell of fairy magic and therefore not seeing with true eyes, he seems a bit foolish laughing at the acted "lovers" in the play. He doesn't know it, but he's still in a play of his own.

Oberon

As king of his magical realm, Oberon is the most powerful figure in the play. Everything about him is commanding, from his language to his magic spells. He is in essence an artist: he knows his craft and how it operates, and he can use his skills to their fullest effect. Since he sets in motion the charmed encounters that are at the heart of the play, he is the author of the plot. The characters play out their dramas to fulfill his needs and wishes. He alone has the overview that an author has.

At times Oberon seems to be almost an elemental, natural force. Because of his quarrel with Titania, the world of nature is completely out of balance. Only a primal power could wreak that kind of havoc on nature. This doesn't mean he is a perfect, all-powerful being. His anger toward Titania has overtones of both jealousy and revenge. You may feel that she has become obsessed with the Indian boy and is neglecting her royal duties as consort of the fairy king, but doesn't Oberon's response seem petulant, maybe a little mean? He is, after all, quite willing to humiliate her and seems to take inordinate joy in it. Yet from the start he is touched by the lovers' plight, and his aim is to unite them, as it is to unite himself and Titania. He knows the power of concord over discord. He isn't all-seeing enough to prevent Puck from making the mistake that brings about the confusion for the lovers, but he knows how to right the wrong that's been done.

Oberon's brilliant poetry is the key to his importance in the play. His speeches contain some of the most extravagant writing in all of Shakespeare. Oberon raises poetry to the level of magic, as if his words were part of his fairy magic lore. He has a commanding knowledge of flowers, which seem to be at the heart of the fairy realm. The dangerous love juice is contained in a flower, as is its antidote. His famous description of Titania's favorite resting place calls out the names of flowers as if just to speak them were to induce a spell. And, indeed, he does induce a spell of poetry. If he describes something, like the Arrow of Cupid striking the flower, or the dawn rising, he does so with such command of detail and sensuality that the scene comes to life before you.

When Oberon finally restores harmony to his relationship with Titania, he seems to do so for everyone else too. Bottom has his ass's head removed in a twinkling, and the lovers are reunited. The wedding of Theseus and Hippolyta can now proceed. The outer edges of the play are held down by the orderly Theseus and Hippolyta, but its inner core burns with the conflict, passion, and magic of the fairy rulers. Theseus mentions that all theater is made up of shadow-plays. When Puck refers to Oberon as the "king of shadows," he's letting us see that as poet and playwright, Oberon is a master of the art.

Titania
Titania is a regal and commanding person. She is not readily willing to give in to the king, and her

insistence on keeping the changeling shows both her strong personal will and the respect she has for her priestess. Though she may lack Oberon's knowledge of magic, she is certainly a primary power like him and has her own court of fairy attendants. She's not about to take any nonsense from him, and she throws his past romantic exploits right in his face. Try to put yourself in her position as well as in Oberon's. What do you think her rights are, especially as a partner in marriage?

Though she may not know the spells, she has the fairy charm. The world she moves in seems to have a special magical grace. She lives among flowers; even her fairy attendants have floral names. Song and dance seem to be the nature of her fairy business. She's not a match for Oberon's magic—he's able to put the doting charm on her. But her world, even more than his, seems to be an enchanted one, delicate, strange, of another dimension and size.

Titania, like Oberon, has the power of poetry. Her description of the natural world in disarray is one of the high points of the play. She seems to invest the disturbed natural forces with her own emotional distress, so that the waves, air, and mud seem to be living, breathing, *personal* things. She knows the range and importance of her and Oberon's power. She may not see that her obsession is as equally to blame as Oberon's jealousy, but she understands the fullest dimensions of the resulting quarrel. Her description of the changeling's mother is a marvel of poetic imagery. The comparison between the pregnant woman and the sails filled with wind makes the world seem filled with a female creative force. Titania embodies that power.

Puck

Jester and jokester, Puck, otherwise known as Robin Goodfellow, is like a wild, untamed member of the fairy clan. Though Oberon tells him they are "spirits of another sort," Puck, with his connection to English legend and folklore, seems related to a slightly more dangerous kind of sprite.

Not that he is truly malevolent. Although his tricks make people uncomfortable, they don't seem to do any permanent damage. He casts an ironic eye on humanity. Thinking people fools, he loves to make fools of them. But laughter, not tears, is his aim. He delights in mischief-making, like a boy bent on fun. He's the childlike antidote to Oberon's seriousness; that's why he's jester as well as jokester.

With his quickness, ventriloquism, and shape-changing ability, he clearly has magic fairy powers of his own. Meddling in the affairs of lovers and administering Cupid's love juice, he's reminiscent of Pan. And like him he seems to have some animal nature. He even tells us that he likes to take the form of animals and that he communicates with them.

He is also reminiscent of the Greek god Hermes, the messenger. Like him, he's a go-between for higher powers. Most of the magic he does in the play is at Oberon's request. He's more the instrument or administerer of magic than the creator of it. He is definitely in the service of Oberon, regarding him with respect and a little fear.

As the liaison between the various groups of characters in the play, Puck is also the character who communicates directly with us, the audience. His swiftness (he can fly around the earth in forty minutes) may give him the ability to cut through dimensions, too. He steps out of the play at the end to suggest that all we've seen may be just a dream—and you can be sure he says it with a wink!

Bottom

Clown, actor, weaver, even romantic hero—Bottom is a complex character. He's able to attract sympathy in the midst of his absurd buffoonery and to elicit concern even though he exhibits some obnoxious qualities. This mix of characteristics has made readers feel many contradictory things about him. Some say he is a boor, that he treats his fellow players with a lack of respect; others note his large ego and need for being in the spotlight. Still other readers find him a perfect clown and take his posturing as harmless joking. He may, of course, reflect all these things. What is your analysis of Bottom?

He is certainly filled with energy; it seems to stream out of him sometimes in ways that he can't stop. He never uses one word when two will do; in the same way, he'd rather not play just one part when he could play them all. Bottom is a ham. He's also a bad actor. The two qualities together make him inevitably funny to us. His enthusiasm trips him up again and again. He is enamored of words. If he misuses or mispronounces them he doesn't notice—though we do. He thinks he knows more than he does know, and it can make him seem arrogant, just as his overabundant energy can make him seem like a bully. But the testimony of his fellow workers makes it clear that they take it all in stride; in fact, they adore him. They seem to appreciate his energy and his acting ability. They're even a little bit in awe of him. And his fondness for them is equally apparent. When he returns to them at last, they are his "lads," his "hearts." The affection these men share is real and touching, especially amid all the confused feelings of love in the rest of the play.

Though he's a bumbler, Bottom also seems to be possessed of a special grace. As a working-class tradesman unaccustomed to finery and delicate manners, his treatment of his fairy servants is a model of courtly behavior. He's not just kind; he's interested in them. He may look like an ass at first glance, but another look reveals something deeper.

Part of his special quality is indicated by the fact that he alone of the mortals actually becomes involved with the fairy world. That Bottom doesn't think Titania's love or dalliance with him is preposterous means he is open to the fairy power in a way no one else is. He may cut a ridiculous figure, wearing an ass's head, but what's interesting is that these strange little creatures don't look ridiculous to him and he's at ease with them as with other persons. When he wakes from his dream, he's unwilling to completely let go of his experience. He feels somehow a joke has been played on him, but he also senses something deeper at the heart of the joke. He tests it on his tongue, savors it, releases it, and calls it back. He's not attached to reason like Theseus, and he does have something of the artist in him. He's willing to absorb his magical experience like a vision and let it find its own meaning. He acts like a fool, but Shakespeare shows us he's not a fool.

Bottom is larger than life. He has a huge appetite. He'd rather engage something than let it go by. He's unself-conscious about both his real abilities and his foibles. That gives him, in the truest sense, a sense of humility. And it's a peculiarity of human nature that humility is ennobling. Bottom's not such a joke, after all.

Quince, Snug, Flute, Snout, and Starveling

These simple folk carve out their own realm in the play, with Bottom at the front. Shakespeare has them speak prose, serving as a sharp contrast to the poetry of the lovers and fairies. They stand as representatives of an innocent real world, plain, good-natured, and well-meaning. Their preposterous bad acting and terrible attempts at poetry are made fun of, but their good intentions and shared fellowship are always apparent. Shakespeare may use them to satirize elements of his theater, but he does so in a way that makes their theatrics, not them, the objects of his comedy. Their burlesque may make them look ridiculous, but as characters they fare better than the more articulate lovers do. They are a necessary adjunct to the other worlds of *A Midsummer Night's Dream*. They counteract the duke's stiff reliance on reason, the lovers' high moral flights of fancy, and the fairies' elegant and primal poetry. All of these realms together make a recognizably human world.

Other Elements
SETTING

Though *A Midsummer Night's Dream* takes place in and around Athens in ancient Greece, you will be hard-pressed to find many details of Greek life. Instead, you will learn much about Elizabethan courtly and country life. While it professes to draw a picture of Athens, the play really seems to take place in England. Puck's descriptions of the tricks he plays on people are filled with details of English village life. And when Titania describes the pestilence and floods that have befallen the countryside since her quarrel with Oberon, she is clearly talking about England, with its manicured gardens and country games.

The real exploration of setting in this play has not so much to do with place as with realms or dimensions of experience. The beginning and the end of the play take place in the city, in the courtly urbane atmosphere of the palace of Theseus, the duke of Athens. It is daylight, and the mood is one of social order and reason. The whole middle of the play, however, takes place in the woods, during a moonlit night. The atmosphere here is one of disorder, of emotional indulgence and magic. ("Wood" was an Elizabethan word for "mad," as Demetrius observes in a pun.) When the characters enter the woods, their emotional lives are put in upheaval. Despite their protestations of rationality (Lysander, for example, pleads this continually), it is the irrational, romantic side of their natures that is revealed. So the two main settings are not just backdrops for the action. They symbolize two different emotional and psychic spheres of experience.

THEMES

Here are some major themes explored by Shakespeare in this play. You will find them explained in greater detail in the scene-by-scene discussion of the novel.

1. TRUE AND FALSE LOVE

The overriding theme of the play deals with the nature of love. Though true love seems to be held up as an ideal, false love is mostly what we are shown. Underneath his frantic comedy, Shakespeare seems to be asking the questions all lovers ask in the throes of their confusion: How do we know when love is real? How can we trust ourselves when we are so easily swayed by passion and by romantic conventions? Some readers sense a bitterness behind the comedy. But you will probably also recognize the truth behind Shakespeare's satire. Often, love leads us down blind alleys and makes us do things we regret later. The lovers in the play—especially the men—are made to seem rather shallow. They change the objects of their affections, all the time swearing eternal love to one or the other. Though marriage is held up at the end as a kind of unifying sacrament, and so gives a picture of a true, sensible, and socially sanctioned love, some critics have found its order a little hollow. The confusion that precedes the weddings seems, somehow, much more to the point.

2. SEEING AND BEING BLIND

From the opening scene, "eyes" and "seeing" are shown to be at the core of how we perceive things in love. Helena says that "love looks not with the eyes but with the mind." In Shakespeare's terms, when lovers are led astray by their feelings they aren't seeing correctly; their eyes are "blind," in the same way we now say that love is blind. Lovers frequently see what they want to, not what is really there. When lovers look with such self-charmed eyes, they are said to be "doting," a key term in the play. Do you know any such doting lovers?

3. WAKING AND DREAMING

All four lovers, plus Bottom and Titania, fall asleep in the course of the play, and all wake up to have themselves or their situations changed. An opposition between waking and dreaming is continually enforced, starting, of course, with the very title of the play. After waking from their final sleep, the lovers feel that their experiences were just dreams. Puck also offers us this explanation in his final monologue: that the play itself was a dream, and that we, the audience, were its slumbering dreamers. Moonlight is associated with dreaming, and daylight with waking. So all the fairy experiences that take place during the moonlit night may be just dreamlike hallucinations. Shakespeare leaves it for you to decide. Which of the experiences do you want to call "real"?

4. REALITY AND ILLUSION

All of the oppositions point toward our perception of reality. And nowhere can that perception be more interestingly tricked than in the theater, which is entirely built on the tension between illusion and reality, shadow and light. Shakespeare teases the audience about its gullibility at the same time he tests it. He makes fun of those who don't think we'd be able to tell the difference between a real or fake lion. He simultaneously charms the audience with a fairy world breathtaking in its magical beauty, making them *want* to believe in the preposterous. The theater is called a place of shadows, but with the right lighting it can come into a life of its own, challenging all our notions about what is real and what illusionary.

5. REASON AND IMAGINATION

Theseus is continually aligned with reason. Sometimes he seems to be held up as a model for social man, clear-sighted (not doting) and responsible. He intentionally sets himself in opposition to the imagination when he compares the lover, the lunatic, and the poet to each other. Their similarity, he says, comes from the fact that they are all swayed by their imaginations. Looking at the sad plight of the lovers, we might agree with Theseus's conclusions. But we can also see that a reliance on reason makes Theseus blind in a different way. The world of the fairies, of magic, mystery, and creative power, is closed to him. Shakespeare says, through Theseus, that the poet "gives to airy nothing/A local habitation and name." Though Theseus seems to say it with scorn, this is exactly what Shakespeare does for us by presenting the airy, spectral fairy world in detailed form. In that case, the workings of the imagination can be seen as something valuable, indeed. Bottom, waking from his dream, seems somehow able to hold the two worlds together. His immediate plan is to make his dream into a song. Perhaps, then, art is the bridge between the world of reason and the world of the imagination. Bottom says this is the power of "vision."

6. CHANGE AND TRANSFORMATION

People are changing their minds, their hearts, and their images throughout the play. The woods become a special arena in which these changes take place. Demetrius and Lysander both change the objects of their affection, triggered by that excellent agent of change, the love juice of Cupid. So love itself is seen as an agent of transformation. It turns people around, and sometimes makes asses of them. That is, of course, exactly what happens to Bottom, though it may seem at times that Titania is the one who has made an ass of herself.

As day changes to night and back again, the fairies present a world transformed by magic, where nothing is what it seems, and everything may evolve into something else.

STYLE

Shakespeare's understanding of a wide range of human experience as well as different levels of consciousness enables him to adapt his style to his characters and their worlds. *A Midsummer Night's Dream* is unique in that its different sets of characters speak in different ways. And their styles of speech tell us things about them.

The ducal court and the romantic lovers speak a conventional courtly poetry, filled with mythical allusions and witty rhetorical gamesmanship. Its conventionality tells us as much about the characters as anything else. The lovers' well-fitted rhymes speak of a complacency, not a creative fire, at the core of their feelings. Note Lysander's first words to Hermia:

"How now, my love! Why is your cheek so
    pale?
How chance the roses there do fade so fast?"
                    (I,i,128–29)

Considering Hermia has just been threatened with death, the rose metaphor seems a little flip. The deeper, threatening emotions of the situation are masked by the poetic rhetoric. But because Shakespeare presents the lovers as comic, not tragic, figures, we can enjoy the intricacy of their metaphors and rhymes while we laugh at their shallowness.

Except for their acted parts in the play at the wedding, the workingmen speak in prose. Shakespeare gives them a sense of being down-to-earth, appropriate to their occupations and simple hearts. When they try to speak poetically, the results are laughable. They continually misuse and mispronounce words, but Shakespeare treats them gently and their simplicity triumphs over their pretensions. Similarly, the silly verse they spout in "Pyramus and Thisby" satirizes bad acting but will probably leave you agreeing with Theseus that the actors' intentions are what matters.

The most eloquent and beautiful poetry in the play belongs to Oberon and Titania. Suddenly you feel the force of real poetry, not its false representatives. Shakespeare clearly aligns his poetry with magic, and Oberon's use of language seems to work like a magic spell. He names flowers with full recognition of their magical potentialities—including the power of the sound of their names.

> "I know a bank where the wild thyme blows,
> Where oxlips and the nodding violet grows,
> Quite overcanopied with luscious woodbine,
> With sweet musk roses, and with eglantine."
> *(II, ii, 249–52)*

This famous passage is really just a list of flowers, but Shakespeare is able to infuse the naming with poetic magic, highlighting the rhythmic and sensual qualities of the language.

ELIZABETHAN ENGLISH

All languages change. Differences in pronunciation and word choice are apparent even between

parents and their children. If language differences
can appear in one generation, it is only to be expected that the English used by Shakespeare four
hundred years ago will differ markedly from the
English used today. The following information on
Shakespeare's language will help a modern reader
to a fuller understanding of *A Midsummer Night's
Dream*.

Mobility of Word Classes

Adjectives, nouns, and verbs were less rigidly confined to particular classes in Shakespeare's day.
Adjectives could be used as adverbs:

> And then the moon, like to a silver bow
> New bent in heaven
>
> *(I,i,9–10)*

"New" is used for "newly." Adjectives could also
be used as nouns:

> Demetrius loves your fair. O happy fair!
>
> *(I,i,182)*

Here, "fair" is the equivalent of "fairness" or
"beauty." Adjectives could also be used as verbs.
"Coy" means "to caress" in

> While I thy amiable cheeks do coy,
>
> *(IV,i,2)*

Nouns could be used as verbs. "Square" means
"to fight, quarrel" in

> But they do square,
>
> *(II,i,30)*

Nouns could also be used as verbals, like "flews"
(dog's jowls) and "sand" (the color of sand) in

My hounds are bred out of the Spartan kind;
So flewed, so sanded;

                              (IV,i,118–19)

Changes in Word Meaning

The meanings of words undergo changes, a process
that can be illustrated by the fact that "silly" used
to mean "holy" and "quick" meant "alive." Most
of the words in Shakespeare's plays still exist today but some meanings have changed. The change
may be small, as in the case of "pert," which meant
"quick to act," as in

Awake the pert and nimble spirit of mirth
                              (I,i,13)

or more fundamental, so that "gossip" *(II,i,47)*
meant "old woman" (possibly a relative), "sad-
dest" *(II,i,51)* meant "most serious," "waxen"
(II,i,56) meant "increase," "weed" *(II,i,256)* meant
"garment, clothes," and "favours" *(IV,i,48)* meant
"flowers given as a token of love."

Vocabulary Loss

Words not only change their meanings but are frequently discarded from the language. In the past,
"leman" meant "sweetheart," "sooth" meant
"truth," and "mewed" meant "confined, cooped
up." The following words used in *A Midsummer
Night's Dream* are no longer current in English, but
their meanings can usually be gauged from the
contexts in which they occur.

   gauds *(I,i,33):* showy toys
   prevailment *(I,i,71):* power
   belike *(I,i,130):* perhaps
   beteem *(I,i,131):* allow

misgraffed *(I,i,137)*: badly matched
collied *(I,i,145)*: darkened
eyne *(I,i,242)*: eyes
an *(I,ii,47)*: if
orbs *(II,i,9)*: fairy rings
lob *(II,i,16)*: fool, clown
fell *(II,i,20)*: fierce
bootless *(II,i,37)*: useless
buskined *(II,i,71)*: wearing hunting clothes
margent *(II,i,85)*: shore
murrion *(II,i,97)*: murrain, disease of animals
Hiems *(II,i,109)*: winter
reremice *(II,ii,4)*: bats
pard *(II,ii,37)*: leopard
owe *(II,ii,85)*: own
by'r lakin *(III,i,12)*: by our lady
ousel or **woosel** *(III,i,118)*: blackbird
throstle *(III,i,120)*: thrush
patches *(III,ii,9)*: clowns
aby *(III,ii,175)*: atone, pay for
welkin *(III,ii,356)*: heavens, sky
wot *(III,ii,422)*: know
neaf *(IV,i,19)*: fist
cry *(IV,i,123)*: pack of hounds
dole *(V,i,270)*: source of sorrow

Verbs

Shakespearean verb forms differ from modern usage in three main ways:

1. Questions and negatives could be formed without using "do/did," as when Oberon asks Titania:

> How long within this wood intend you stay?
> *(II,i,138)*

where today we would say, "How long do you
intend to stay?" or as when Demetrius tells Helen:

> I love thee not, therefore pursue me not.
> *(II,i,189)*

where modern usage demands, "I do not love you,
so don't follow me."

Shakespeare had the option of using forms (a)
or (b), whereas contemporary usage permits only
the (a) forms:

(a)	(b)
What are you saying?	What say you?
What did you say?	What said you?
I do not love you.	I love you not.
I did not love you.	I loved you not.

2.   A number of past participles and past tense
forms are used that would be ungrammatical today. Among these are "broke" for "broken":

> By all the vows that ever men have broke,
> *(I,i,175)*

"forgot" for "forgotten":

> And—to speak truth—I have forgot our way.
> *(II,ii,42)*

"afeared" for "afraid":

> Will not the ladies be afeard of the lion?
> *(III,i,25)*

"mistook" for "mistaken":

> And the youth mistook by me,
> *(III,ii,112)*

and "writ" for "wrote":

> Marry, if he that writ it had played
> Pyramus . . .
>
> *(V,i,348)*

3.   Archaic verb forms sometimes occur with "thou" and with third person subjects:

> Thou shalt remain here, whether thou wilt or
> no.
>
> *(III,i,144)*

> Music, ho! Music such as charmeth sleep!
> *(IV,1,82)*

> And all their minds transfigured so together,
> More witnesseth than fancy's images,
> *(V,i,24–25)*

Pronouns

Shakespeare and his contemporaries had one extra pronoun, "thou," which could be used in addressing a person who was one's equal or social inferior. "You" was obligatory if more than one person was addressed, so "you" is used when Puck addresses the audience:

> Think but this, and all is mended:
> That you have but slumbered here,
>
> *(V,i,414–15)*

but it could also be used to indicate respect. Lysander and Hermia show their respect for each other by using "you":

> *Lys.*   Fair love, you faint with wandering in the
>   wood;
>   . . . .
> *Her.*   Be it so, Lysander; find you out a bed,
>   For I upon this bank will rest my head.
>   *(II,ii,41ff)*

Frequently, a person in power used "thou" to a

child or a subordinate but was addressed "you" in
return, as when Oberon speaks to Puck:

> *Obe.*   And look thou meet me ere the first cock
>   crow.
> *Puck*   Fear not, my lord, your servant shall do
>   so.
>
> *(II,i,267–68)*

but if "thou" was used inappropriately it could
cause grave offense. Oberon intended to offend
Titania when he addressed her as "thou":

> How canst thou thus, for shame, Titania,
>
> *(II,i,74)*

Prepositions

Prepositions were less standardized in Elizabethan
English than they are today and so we find several
uses in *A Midsummer Night's Dream* that would have
to be modified in contemporary speech. Among
these are
"in" for "on":

> Or in the beached margent of the sea,
>
> *(II,i,85)*

"upon" for "by":

> To die upon the hand I love so well.
>
> *(II,i,244)*

"on" for "of":

> More fond on her than she upon her love:
>
> *(II,i,266)*

"against" for "in anticipation of":

> And now have toiled their unbreathed memo-
> ries

With this same play against your nuptial.
(V,i,74–75)

and "to" for "in":

In least speak most, to my capacity.
(V,i,105)

Multiple Negation

Contemporary English requires only one negative per statement and regards such utterances as "I haven't none" as nonstandard. However, Shakespeare often used two or more negatives for emphasis, as when Helena chides Lysander:

Is't not enough, is't not enough, young man,
That I did never—no, nor never can—
Deserve a sweet look from Demetrius' eye,
(II,ii,131ff)

and Bottom agrees with Titania:

Not so neither;
(III,i,141)

POINT OF VIEW

Though a playwright does not generally have an all-seeing or subjective voice to speak from, he does have characters to represent various points of view. But can you always tell what Shakespeare himself feels about things in *A Midsummer Night's Dream*? Do his characters speak for him? Or do you feel that he sometimes disappears behind his characters, making the reader decide what to feel about the issues?

Theseus is the voice for reason, for civil order and the mature subjugation of romantic passion in marriage. The four lovers, on the other hand, speak out for romance. Since their interactions are the basis of the comedy, and since they are all married in the end, they too make us feel the frivolity of romance. But Oberon, Titania, and Puck keep things from getting too structured or domestic. In them we feel authentic wild powers, a force of nature (we might call it magic) that need not be tamed. This natural force is also aligned with art. These different forces keep us from settling too easily into judgments about love and reason.

By presenting us with two distinct worlds—the courtly domain of order and the wild woods—Shakespeare also shows us the necessity for a balance between the two. Neither one will suffice alone. Theseus seems too constricted by reason, the lovers too driven and distracted by emotion. You may feel sympathetic with all the different characters and levels of experience of the play. Shakespeare's architecture seems to insist that all together are necessary for a rounded view of our world.

FORM AND STRUCTURE

Though Shakespeare's plays are now divided for us into acts and scenes, these are very likely the work of later editors. We do not really know where Shakespeare's players made their pauses. The Elizabethan stage was so bare and fluid that it wasn't necessary to stop frequently for scene or costume changes, as it is today. It's more interesting to look at the play itself to get a sense of form and structure.

The play has a very simple time architecture. Most of the action takes place during one long frantic

The Five-act Structure

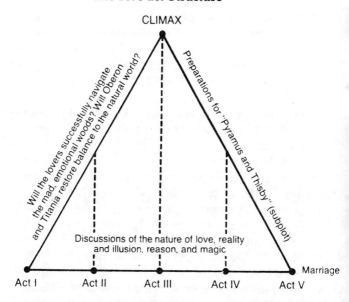

CLIMAX

Will the lovers successfully navigate the mad, emotional woods? Will Oberon and Titania restore balance to the natural world?

Preparations for "Pyramus and Thisby" (subplot)

Discussions of the nature of love, reality and illusion, reason, and magic

Act I — Act II — Act III — Act IV — Act V — Marriage

Act I: Exposition. The problem with the four lovers is revealed. They each seem to be in love with the wrong person.

Act II: Rising Action. The quarrel between Oberon and Titania intensifies. Lysander is given the love juice.

Act III: Climax. Oberon's plan works: Bottom is transformed and Titania humiliated. The lovers are in complete disarray.

Act IV: Falling Action. The lovers, Titania, and Bottom wake up from their "dreams." Oberon and Titania are reconciled.

Act V: Resolution. The three couples prepare for marriage, and the play within the play is performed, exorcising the tragic element in favor of the comic.

night, framed at either end by a brief spate of day. And time parallels place. The play opens at court, in the sunny, rational, social world of Theseus the duke. The main course of the play takes place in the Athenian woods outside of town. There it is night—a mysterious world filled with spirits and human passions. At the end we are in court again. Day has returned, the order of marriage is triumphant, and the bonds of the social world are re-strengthened.

You might also find structural beauty in the way Shakespeare juggles the four realms his characters inhabit. By the way they speak and the kinds of characters they reveal, the people in the play seem to occupy distinct realms or zones of existence, which Shakespeare interweaves throughout the play. Theseus and Hippolyta, as members of the royal court, live in an extremely social world and stand for the orderly workings of society. The four lovers, in their travels from court to wood and back to court again, exist in a realm governed by the passions, and so come to stand for man's volatile emotional life. The rustic workingmen, with their simple trades, physical comedy, and earthy sensibilities, represent the material world. And the fairies—delicate, mysterious, elemental, with creative power and poetic art—represent the world of the spirit. All these worlds exist simultaneously. Shakespeare means us to see that the structure they combine to create is the human universe.

SOURCES

As with most of his plays, Shakespeare drew on many different sources to help shape *A Mid-*

summer Night's Dream. There does not seem to be an earlier plot that he incorporated—rather, a series of myths and tales that he drew from to create his own work. But most of our understanding of Shakespearean sources is like detective work: we piece together similarities but we have no direct testimony.

Sir Thomas North's translation of Plutarch's *Life of Theseus* seems to have given Shakespeare some of the mythical background for the play, particularly relating to Theseus's past exploits, romantic and otherwise. The name Egeus (Hermia's father) probably also came from Plutarch.

Shakespeare seems almost certain to have borrowed some information from the fourteenth-century poet Geoffrey Chaucer, whose "Knight's Tale," in the *Canterbury Tales,* opens with lines about Theseus and Hippolyta. It also mentions observances of May Day.

Similarly, Ovid's *Metamorphosis,* translated by Arthur Golding, gave Shakespeare a very clear working of the story of Pyramus and Thisby. This is probably where Shakespeare picked up his word "cranny," through which the unfortunate lovers are forced to speak.

And it is also likely that Shakespeare knew of the Roman writer Apuleius's story *The Golden Ass.* In it a poor man is transformed by enchantment into an ass. In the description of the transformation, there are many similar phrases that tie the two together.

For his fairies, Shakespeare had a vast store of folklore to draw on. Robin Goodfellow was particularly well-known in country lore, though Shakespeare may have been the first to give him the name of Puck. May Day (May 1) and Midsummer's Night (June 23/summer solstice) were two festivals important as background for the play. May Day (when *A Midsummer Night's Dream* actually takes place) was a favorite festival for rural England, a time in which the people left the city and headed for the woods, where they danced and celebrated. A king and queen of May were elected, and this "royal" couple went to the nobles' houses to give their blessings, much the way Oberon and Titania do at the end of the play. May Day was, above all, a time of lovers' madness: they, too, went to the woods and frequently spent the night there. Midsummer was a general celebration of madness and merriment, a time when magic was afoot and the fairies were particularly evident. Costumes and dancing played a large part in the festivities. "Midsummer madness," brought about by the heat, affected everyone, opening the way for illusion (and delusion) to transform reality.

Shakespeare even drew on some of his own work. The situation of the workmen awkwardly performing their amateur theatricals is similar to the show of the Nine Worthies in *Love's Labour's Lost*. In *Two Gentlemen of Verona*, the way that couples mix up and transfer their affections is reminiscent of the *Midsummer* lovers. And if *Romeo and Juliet* was, as is often suggested, written directly before *A Midsummer Night's Dream*, it offers an entrance into the fairy world with Mercutio's famous description of Queen Mab.

THE GLOBE THEATRE

One of the most famous theaters of all time is the Globe Theatre. It was one of several Shakespeare worked in during his career, and many of the greatest plays of English literature were performed there. Built in 1599 for £600 just across the River Thames from London, it burned down in 1613 when a spark from one of the cannons in a battle scene in Shakespeare's *Henry VIII* set fire to the thatched roof. The theater was quickly rebuilt and survived until 1644. No one knows exactly what the Globe looked like but some scholarly detective work has given us a fairly good idea. The Folger Shakespeare Library in Washington, D.C., has a full scale re-creation of the Globe.

When it was built, the Globe was the latest thing in theater design. It was a three-story octagon, with covered galleries surrounding an open yard some 50 feet across. Three sides of the octagon were devoted to the stage and backstage areas. The main stage was a raised platform that jutted into the center of the yard, or pit. Behind the stage was the tiring house—the backstage area where the actors dressed and waited for their cues. This area was flanked by two doors and contained an inner stage, with a curtain that was used when the script called for a scene to be discovered. (Some scholars think the inner stage was actually a tent or pavillion that could be moved about the stage.) Above the inner stage was the upper stage, a curtained balcony that could serve as the battlements in *Hamlet* or for the balcony scene in *Romeo and Juliet*. Most of the action of the play took place on the main and upper stages.

The third story held the musicians' gallery and machinery for sound effects and pyrotechnics. Above all was a turret from which a flag was flown to announce, "Performance today." A roof (the

GLOBE THEATRE

the shadow
upper stage
doors
tiring house
inner stage
main stage
trapdoor
tower
musicians' gallery
orchestra
galleries
yard or pit

shadow) covered much of the stage and not only protected the players from sudden showers but also contained machinery needed for special effects. More machinery was under the stage, where several trapdoors permitted the sudden appearance in a play of ghosts and allowed actors to leap into rivers or graves, as the script required.

For a penny (a day's wages for an apprentice), you could stand with the "groundlings" in the yard to watch the play; another penny would buy you a seat in the upper galleries, and a third would get you a cushioned seat in the lower gallery—the best seats in the house. The audience would be a mixed crowd—sedate scholars, gallant courtiers, and respectable merchants and their families in the galleries; rowdy apprentices and young men looking for excitement in the yard; and pickpockets and prostitutes taking advantage of the crowds to ply their trades. And crowds there would be—the Globe could probably hold 2000 to 3000 people, and even an ordinary performance would attract a crowd of 1200.

The play would be performed in broad daylight during the warmer months. In colder weather, Shakespeare's troupe appeared indoors at Court or in one of London's private theaters. There was no scenery as we know it, but there are indications that the Elizabethans used simple set pieces such as trees, bowers, or battle tents to indicate location. Any props needed were readied in the tiring house by the book keeper (we'd call him the stage manager) and carried on and off by actors. If time or location were important, the characters usually said something about it. Trumpet flourishes told the audience an important character was about to enter, rather like a modern spotlight, and a scene ended when all the characters left the stage. (Bodies of dead characters were carried off stage.) Little attention was paid to historical accuracy in plays such as *Julius Caesar* or *Macbeth*, and actors wore contemporary clothing. One major difference from the modern theater was that all female parts were played by young boys; Elizabethan custom did not permit women to act.

If the scenery was minimal, the performance made up for it in costumes and spectacle. English actors were famous throughout Europe for their skill as dancers, and some performances ended with a dance (or jig). Blood, in the form of animal blood or red paint, was lavished about in the tragedies; ghosts made sudden appearances amidst swirling fog; thunder was simulated by rolling a cannon ball along the wooden floor of the turret or by rattling a metal sheet. The costumes were gorgeous— and expensive! One "robe of estate" alone cost £19, a year's wages for a skilled workman of the time. But the costumes were a large part of the spectacle that the audience came to see, and they had to look impressive in broad daylight, with the audience right up close.

You've learned some of the conventions of the Globe Theatre, a theater much simpler than many of ours but nevertheless offering Shakespeare a wide range of possibilities for staging his plays. Now let's see how specific parts of *A Midsummer Night's Dream* might have been presented at the Globe.

A Midsummer Night's Dream is unusual in that it takes almost no advantage of the multiple stages available to Shakespeare at the Globe. This may well be because the play was originally written to be performed privately as part of the celebrations of a particular wedding, and moved to the public theater later. Almost all the action takes place in the woods near Athens, and all of it could be performed on the main stage. The setting is, however, one of the most popular for Elizabethan plays—a woods. There may have been some standard props brought in to suggest a forest scene, or the actors may just have treated the pillars as if they were trees.

You can see how the absence of scenery and lighting affects the play, though. The characters are constantly mentioning that now it is nighttime and that they are in the woods. If they didn't say so, how could the audience know? (In this play, nighttime is particularly important for many of the scenes, because that is when the fairies are in charge.)

The ending of the play is also typically Elizabethan. Since there was no curtain to fall, there were different conventions: tragedies frequently ended with a funeral march and bodies being carried off the stage, while comedies ended the way *A Midsummer Night's Dream* does, with music and a dance.

The Play

ACT I

ACT I, SCENE I

Lines 1–127

The scene is the palace of Theseus, duke of Athens. He is preparing to wed Hippolyta, queen of the Amazons, a famous tribe of women warriors. She had earlier been taken captive by Theseus. They are both legendary figures, and their speeches and actions have a kind of formality. But like any husband-to-be, Theseus is anxious for the wedding day, which will be marked by a new moon. It is still five days away, and Theseus complains about how slowly the old moon wanes. Hippolyta reminds him that the four nights will be filled with dreams that will quickly pass the time. Theseus sends Philostrate, his master of the revels (a kind of entertainment coordinator), to prepare the festivities for the wedding celebration.

NOTE: The moon   From the very beginning, the moon shines forth as the main image of the play. Its mood and its mystical connections tie the various subplots together. The word *moon* appears twenty-eight times in the play, passing through its phases and working its magic. For Theseus and Hippolyta the moon is the means of measuring the time till their wedding day, and so, in a way, it is the light that illumines their marriage. It also lights the woods for the eloping lovers, Hermia and Lysander, and because of its nighttime appearance is associated with romance. Moonlight is the fairies' proper illumination; they are creatures of the night world and revel under the moon's magic, spectral beams. Even for the rustics, the workingmen, the moon is important. It is, in fact, one of the "characters" in their play, as it shines over the garden in which Pyramus and Thisby secretly meet. And, especially, the moon symbolizes the night, in which dreams take place, as well as the mad, bewitching

Midsummer's Eve, in which dreams and reality intermingle.

Egeus, an Athenian elder, enters, followed by his daughter Hermia and her two suitors, Lysander and Demetrius. Egeus is extremely upset. He tells Theseus that he has given consent to Demetrius to marry his daughter. However, Hermia is of a different mind. Egeus explains that Lysander has "bewitched" Hermia with poetry, song, and lovers' trinkets so that she wants to marry him and not Demetrius. Athenian law says the father has the right to marry off his daughter as he sees fit— or have her put to death for her disobedience. Egeus asks Theseus to uphold that law. Notice how the sweet order of marriage established in the opening lines between Theseus and Hippolyta has immediately been disrupted. Now there is romantic discord instead of harmony, and the contrast between the two will run throughout the play. The conflict has been set up between love and law (or reason, as it is later called).

Theseus questions Hermia, explaining that a daughter must obey her father. Hermia, adamant in her refusal, says she wishes her father would look with *her* eyes, but Theseus chides her, saying that she must learn to see with her father's eyes. She asks to know the worst that can happen to her if she defies Egeus. Theseus explains that she must either give up men and enter a nunnery, or else be put to death. As you can see, the stakes in this romantic discord are very high. Put yourself in Hermia's position. Can you sympathize with her problem? The proper behavior in love is sometimes hard to decide; having to choose between a father and two different suitors makes the decision even harder. If Hermia were to ask your advice, what would you say to her?

NOTE: Shakespeare is a poet as well as a playwright, and that means much of his information is conveyed through imagery as well as action. Watch carefully the ways in which "eyes" and "seeing" function throughout the play. You may be reminded of the old saying, "Beauty is in the eye of the beholder." Our eyes are only one way of judging reality, and they can be easily fooled. Especially in romantic love, where appearances are so important, how can we be sure of what we're feeling (seeing)? *A Midsummer Night's Dream* is concerned with multiple layers of reality. Note the ways in which peoples' eyes fool them.

Hermia absolutely refuses to marry Demetrius. Theseus gives her until the next new moon—his wedding day—to decide her own fate. Lysander protests that he is as worthy as Demetrius and is, in any event, loved by Hermia. He can't resist throwing in that Demetrius had previously sought and won the love of Helena. Therefore, why doesn't he marry *her?* But the law is the law. Theseus gives Hermia one more warning, and the rest exit, leaving her and Lysander alone.

Lines 128–251
The two frustrated lovers try to comfort each other. They speak in a poetic, almost courtly manner,

trading clever lines and poetic imagery back and forth. The style reflects the content here. They speak the way conventional romantic characters do. But how appropriate is that to their current situation, dangerous and distressing as it is? Does their reliance on stock romantic speech get in the way of their real feelings, instead of express them? What's real or true is hard to see and, as Lysander explains, "the course of true love never did run smooth." "O hell!" responds Hermia, sticking with her theme, "To choose love by another's eyes!" Both feel that happiness in love is fleeting, but agree to take the challenge of making it endure.

Lysander tells Hermia of a secret plan. He has an aunt who lives outside Athens and who looks on him as a son. Lysander proposes that he and Hermia flee the city and live together in marriage at his aunt's house, free from the cruel Athenian law. Both agree to meet the following night in the woods outside of town and to put their plan of elopement into action. Hermia swears repeatedly that she will meet Lysander there. She gets carried away in her romantic poetic flight, swearing by several "broken" vows as well as true ones. We understand what she's saying, but her examples don't really inspire much confidence in the success of romantic entanglement. In spite of the possible deadly consequences of the couple's actions, Shakespeare is reminding us we are in a comic situation.

Suddenly Helena enters, the picture of frustration. Where Hermia and Lysander are caught up in their mutual love, Helena bears testimony for love's other side, its false side. She is miserable that Demetrius loves Hermia rather than her, and explains how she would willingly change places with Hermia, wishing her voice could be Hermia's and "my eye your eye."

But Helena and Hermia do not trade places. Instead, they trade rhymed lines back and forth, comparing their situations. Hermia frowns on Demetrius, who nevertheless still loves her; Helena wishes her smiles could elicit such a good reaction. Hermia curses him and still he loves her; Helena wishes her prayers could bring the same results. Their romantic plight, signaled by the high poetic style, is undercut by the perfect fit of their comically mismatched desires.

NOTE: The four lovers   Many readers have complained that the four Athenian lovers are difficult to tell apart and are not very richly characterized. It may be that the ways in which they are alike are more important than the ways in which they are different. Watch how they become even more interchangeable through the course of the play. Do you think they are meant to represent lovers in general, rather than four particular people?

Though Hermia and Helena are drawn as opposites, we do not get very much physical or emotional detail about them. But their situation highlights their opposition, their differences. They are connected by, yet also placed in opposition by, their mutually frustrated desires. In the passage about Demetrius, the end rhymes make us feel the young women are connected, yet the fact that one has what she doesn't want but the other does shows us how they are opposed. That they are lovers aligns them. Love's inconstancy sets them apart.

The plot gives them their definition: they are alternately frustrated and mated.

To give Helena a little comfort—and a little hope—Hermia tells her of their plan to elope. Lysander explains that when the moon rises the next night (the moon is to light their way, but its enchanted beams can mislead as well as lead, as they will discover), he and Hermia will leave the city. Helena knows the meeting place. She and Hermia used to play and embroider there as children and opened their hearts to each other. Shakespeare reminds you, with these details of their past, that there are several kinds of love. The love the two women shared as children will be tested by the new love they both now seek. Lysander and Hermia exit.

Helena is left alone with her unhappiness and is quick to spell it out for you. Imagine yourself in Helena's position. How would your frustration color your thoughts? Her soliloquy is worth examining closely because in it she touches on several of the play's themes. First Helena complains that throughout Athens she is thought to be as pretty as Hermia. Why doesn't Demetrius agree? He, instead, dotes on "Hermia's eyes." Here the problem with seeing is doubled: eyes can bewitch eyes. Demetrius can no longer see what everyone else in Athens can. But Helena is in a similar predicament. Though she resents Demetrius, she also loves him. Why?

> Things base and vile, holding no quantity,
> Love can transpose to form and dignity.
> $\qquad$ (I,i,232–33)

The eyes of love are selective and transforming.

They can see beauty where beauty is, but they can also mistake ugliness for beauty. Keep this power of love in mind; Titania will be seriously under its influence when she confronts Bottom wearing his ass's head.

But love is even more complex than that. In fact, says Helena, love doesn't see "with the eyes, but with the mind." And that is why Cupid is said to be blind, shooting his arrows aimlessly. The eyes of lovers do not merely transform the object of their desire; sometimes they don't really see it at all! (That is Demetrius' problem with Helena. He can no longer see her.) And, adds Helena, love is a child because it can be so easily "beguiled." All the oaths that Demetrius once swore to Helena are worth nothing now. The way Helena describes it, love is something like looking in a hall of mirrors. There are reflections behind reflections behind reflections, and it's not easy to tell the real from the false. The lover's eyes can see what isn't there, yet not see what is there. The mind can play tricks on the eyes, and the eyes, on the mind. Most importantly, love has the power to transform. Under its rule, appearance and reality become one. This idea recurs throughout the entire play (if you can only *see* it!).

NOTE: Another thing that challenges our perceptions about appearance and reality is the theater itself. If you keep in mind that, ideally, you would be watching a play instead of reading it, you will be able to appreciate another layer of meaning in *A Midsummer Night's Dream*. The theater, like romantic love, has the power to enchant our eyes and transform what we see.

ACT I, SCENE II

We are now in another part of Athens, in the house of Quince, a carpenter. He and his comrades—Snug, a joiner; Bottom, a weaver; Flute, a bellows mender; Snout, a tinker; and Starveling, a tailor—have gathered together to choose the parts in a play they'll be performing for the duke's wedding. They're a group of simple working people, not professional actors, and they're also a far cry from any traditional image of noble Athenian youth.

NOTE: Unlike the lovers, the rustics speak in prose, which is appropriate to their more mundane station in life. But like the lovers, the way they speak tells us a lot about who they are. They're not particularly literate people, so dramatic dialogue isn't very comfortable for them. Watch the way they try to impress or outdo each other, particularly Bottom, who feels he can undertake any part.

Quince asks if all the company is assembled to rehearse. Bottom says it would be better to call all the names individually, but he uses the word "generally" instead. This is one of Bottom's characteristic traits. He has more enthusiasm than knowledge and is a true ham. He loves to use big words even if he doesn't really understand them. He is infatuated with the sound and the flourish of them. But he approaches language with such relish and gusto that it's hard to fault him. He may not always be correct, but his heart is in the right place. Shakespeare knows enough about language to show us that a word's sound can often override its sense. Even when Bottom's wrong, he often *sounds* right to us (as he does to himself), so Shakespeare's joke is on us as well as on Bottom. Did you ever try to impress anyone by trying to use a larger word than you could handle? If you got away with it, were you or your listener the greater fool?

Bottom also recommends that Quince tell the name of the play first, and so we discover the piece to be presented is "The most lamentable comedy, and most cruel death of Pyramus and Thisby." Its very title gives you a good indication of its contradictory nature: "lamentable" but a "comedy." It might also indicate to you how little these actors really know about the theater. Obviously, this is going to be a chance for Shakespeare—a trained actor as well as playwright—to give us some inside jokes.

NOTE: The story of Pyramus and Thisby is not Shakespeare's invention; it was a stock Elizabethan plot. But notice how cleverly it fits into *A Midsummer Night's Dream*. The play within the play concerns two lovers frustrated by their parents' interference. We have just seen a similar situation with Hermia, Lysander, and Egeus. Shakespeare will make great comic use of this traditional story line to comment on the actions of his own characters.

Bottom is the first up. When told that his part is to be Pyramus, Bottom wants to know if Pyramus is a lover or a tyrant. His appetite is large, and he is ready to bite into a big part and give it his full dramatic powers. The part, explains Quince, is that of a "lover that kills himself, most gallant, for love." Quince recognizes Bottom's need for the large gesture. He adds the words "most gallant" like food for Bottom's appetite.

Bottom understands the depths of the dramatic task at hand and immediately begins pumping himself up for it. He sees that such a tragic figure will require great poignance in order both to shed tears (as Pyramus) and to bring the audience to compassionate tears of their own. "I will move storms," he assures his fellows. However, he adds, he *could* well play a tyrant if asked to do so—and then to prove it, he does so. Bottom is a one-man band. Though some readers have felt he is at times egotistical or overbearing, others note his eagerness to grab onto life and play it to the hilt. Certainly, Bottom doesn't let much pass him by. If he won't be able to play a tyrant in "Pyramus and Thisby," he'll play it right now for us. He digs into his speech with total energy. The too-obvious alliteration ("raging rocks," "shivering shocks") and high-blown poetic rhetoric don't matter. Their overly conscious style may be appropriate for a tyrant anyway. What does matter is Bottom's enthusiasm. He puts on these parts and takes them off

with utter relish. He really enjoys being the center
of attention. And he is thoroughly pleased with
his own powers. After his speech—almost like
coming out of a trance—he admits, "This was lofty!"

Next up is Francis Flute. His part is to be Thisby.
Flute wonders naively—hopefully—if that's the part
of a wandering knight. No such luck; Thisby is
Pyramus's lady love. Flute protests: Can't he play
someone else? He has a beard coming. (Mind you
it's not here, but it's coming.) But that's his assigned part, and Quince assures him he can play
it behind a mask, speaking "small" (softly).

NOTE: Did you know that all female roles in
Elizabethan theater were played by boys or young
men? Women were not allowed on the stage. The
profession of acting was still seen as a socially inferior—if not immoral—occupation. Since that was
the law, men performing as women was socially
accepted at the time. However, Flute is disturbed
at being assigned Thisby's role because he wants
to imagine himself a man rather than a boy (not
because he's worried about playing a woman),
though we can certainly guess a good deal of jesting took place in Shakespeare's time around the
issue.

If Flute is reluctant to play the part, someone
else is always ready. That someone, of course, is
Bottom, always within dramatic arm's reach. He
offers to play the role, speaking in a "monstrous
little voice." As is often the case, Bottom combines

inappropriate words ("monstrous" and "little") to convey his meaning, but the ingenuity and verve of this man, who can quickly swoop from raging tyrant to sweet Thisby is amazing.

Quince, a resourceful and commanding fellow, has things well in hand. Bottom must play Pyramus; Flute, Thisby; Starveling, Thisby's mother; Snout, Pyramus's father; and Quince himself, Thisby's father. (These parts mysteriously disappear in the final version of the play as it is performed. The players may have discovered that their talents or energy were more limited than at first surmised.) In addition, Snug will play the lion's part. Snug is a little worried. He asks Quince if the lion's part is already written so that he may study it now—he's a bit slow at learning. Quince explains handily that Snug can do the part extemporaneously, for it is "nothing but roaring."

Sensing an opening in Snug's reluctance, Bottom makes his move. He's ready to play the lion, and if given the opportunity he will really roar. Quince warns that too realistic roaring would frighten the court ladies, and then they'd all be in trouble. Bottom accommodates; in that case he will roar as gently as a dove or a nightingale. Does that make sense? It doesn't matter. His unquenchable zest is what matters to Bottom.

Quince holds to his position. Bottom must play only Pyramus. But Quince, as director, is no fool. He knows how to butter up his temperamental crew. He flatters Bottom by explaining how appropriate the part is for him—"sweet-faced," "proper," and "gentlemanlike." Bottom is caught but not stopped. He wants to know what kind of beard he should wear and shows off his masterly weaver's knowledge of color by offering an inventory of possible beards.

Quince gives his final orders: they will meet the next night in the palace wood about a mile outside of town by—of course—"moonlight." Quince will draw up a list of the stage properties needed. Bottom gets in a last lick. He repeats the pledge to meet, adding the comment that they will be able to rehearse "most obscenely and courageously." He's used the wrong words again, loving the pure sound of his speech.

As he departs, he adds the line "hold or cut bowstrings." This odd phrase has confused many readers. It's not entirely clear what the expression means, though it seems to be akin to our American "fish or cut bait." Even more likely, he has just garbled some Elizabethan colloquial phrase.

ACT II

ACT II, SCENE I

Lines 1–59

In a wood near Athens, the very same one mentioned in the previous act, two fairies appear. Puck, also known as Robin Goodfellow, asks the other sprite what she's up to. The fairy explains her activities. She wanders throughout the countryside, swifter than the moon, as an attendant of the fairy queen, Titania. Her mission at the moment is to place dew on the flowers. The cowslips (a yellow wildflower) are the queen's personal bodyguards, and the fairy is going to place a drop of dew in the "ear" of each, like a pearl.

NOTE: The fairies The fairies introduce another realm in this play of transformations and inter-locking zones of reality. Shakespeare immediately gives us a clue to their other-worldly nature by associating them with flowers. Shakespeare drew on many traditions in the creation of his fairy folk. Midsummer's Eve was a customary time for strange happenings (midsummer madness it was called) and was associated in folklore with fairy people, as well as with general dancing and cavorting through the woods. Some critics feel that the tiny flower-sized fairies are Shakespeare's invention. It is also likely, though, that there were oral tradi-tions of such creatures that he drew on. What is certain is that ever since Shakespeare wrote of them, his tiny spirits have created their own tradition, so that is how we tend to think of them even today. Note, however, that Oberon and Titania seem to be of human scale, so you might read Shake-speare's playing with the size of the fairies as a way of placing them in a strange other-worldly context.

The fairy must get on with her work, as the queen and her elves will be arriving shortly. This worries Puck. The king, Oberon, is also coming that eve-ning, and it's important the king and queen don't meet. They have had a falling-out that is setting the natural world on edge. Titania has a little In-dian boy as an attendant. He is the son of one of her mortal worshipers or "votaries," and the queen has given him special attention, crowning him with flowers and taking him everywhere with her. (The boy is described as a "changeling," traditionally a child left by the fairies in exchange for one they have stolen.) Oberon is furiously jealous. He'd like this child to be in *his* train. The situation between the two has become so intense that anytime they meet of late they clash so violently that the elves crawl into acorn cups for fear.

Suddenly the fairy thinks she recognizes Puck. Isn't he the sprite also called Robin Goodfellow, who plays pranks on the villagers? This Robin has been known to mischievously interfere with the milling process, to make the housewife churn her butter in vain, to see that drink doesn't ferment properly, and generally to mislead people. Yes, answers Puck, he is that very same Hobgoblin, jester and companion to Oberon. He's a trickster all right. He doesn't really hurt people, but he loves to have fun at their expense. Do you know of someone like this? He can fool horses by neighing like a mare; he can pose as a crabapple bobbing in a drink and make it spill over the old woman drinking it. Sometimes he'll even pretend to be a stool—sit on him and down you go!

NOTE: Puck or Robin Goodfellow also had a rich tradition in folklore. He could be helpful as well as mischievous, though he seemed to prefer the latter. Puck is actually a general term for a spirit, often called "the pook." Notice how thoroughly English his world is, a true country village. There's nothing much Athenian in it. Shakespeare seems content to call the place Athens, but to let the details speak of England. One contemporary of Shakespeare's, however, Thomas Nashe, suggested that the English elves and pooks were the counterpart to the Greek satyrs and nymphs, so that though the specific figures were different, the magical, mythical world was similar.

Lines 60–187
The chatter between Puck and the fairy is ended by the sudden appearance of Oberon at one end of the stage and Titania at the other. The mood, as suggested by Puck, is dark and angry. "Ill met by moonlight, proud Titania" is Oberon's welcome. The moon's light, which is generally their natural accustomed light, has turned sour. This king and queen are in a mutual rage—his, a jealous one, as Titania points out. She is ready to leave immediately. Oberon upbraids her; is he not her lord? But Titania is not the kind of woman who can be easily pushed around. If he is her lord, she asks, why has he gone running around with Phillida (a familiar figure in romantic poetry)? And not only that—isn't the real reason he's come to Athens so that he can bless the union of Theseus and Hippolyta, his "former mistress" and "warrior love"? Obviously, the jealousy works both ways. Try to understand both of their sides. Is Oberon being too domineering? Is Titania neglecting her duties? Oberon and Titania are not nice "airy sprites" or tiny, funny elves. They are both mighty magical powers. They rule over an enchanted and mysterious realm, and they are filled with intelligence, passion, and cunning. They have the full range of human emotions, but their power is more than human. Oberon throws back his accusations: Titania is herself in love with Theseus and has pre-

viously caused the duke to break off with other of his affairs.

Titania, exasperated, replies that all of that has been concocted by Oberon's jealous imagination. Ever since the beginning of midsummer, Oberon has spoiled all their meetings with his jealous rages. More than that: this disturbance between them has set the whole natural world out of order. The primal forces themselves seem to be taking revenge on the king and queen who are so furiously at odds. The winds have sucked up fogs from the sea and overswollen the rivers with their contents. The ox and the farmer have labored in vain; the grain is rotting in the drowned field. The cattle are dead and the crows fat from feeding off them. The lovely English mazes and lawn games are full of mud. Even the moon is so angry that she spreads diseases through the air. The picture is absolutely frightening. It's almost as if biblical plagues have descended on England, corrupting its beauty. The very seasons are out of whack. Nobody can tell whether it's summer or winter. Frost falls on the new rose and spring buds burst through the snow and ice. And all of this, explains Titania, has occurred because she and Oberon have lost their harmony.

NOTE: This confusion in the natural world indicates how powerful Oberon and Titania are. You all know how difficult a family disturbance can be; sometimes it feels as if the whole world is breaking apart. But with Oberon and Titania it seems to be literally true. That their quarrel affects nature also displays the ways in which the different realms of the play affect each other. Each set of characters (the court, the lovers, the fairies, and the rustics) reflects and comments upon the others.

Titania's speech contains some of the most beautiful language in the play. Part of the excitement in experiencing Shakespeare is in noticing how rich his writing is, how fully he explores and expands his images and brings them to life. To really make the natural disasters vivid, he uses personification. All the forces of the world seem to act with will and emotion, just as people do. The wind sucks up water from the sea "as in revenge"; the rivers overflow because they are "proud"; the moon is "pale in her anger." The whole scene, then, is alive with feeling. And when things have feeling, don't you have stronger feelings for them?

Oberon tells Titania it's within her power to restore order to the world: all she has to do is give the changeling boy to him. Titania is not interested. She explains how close she was to the boy's mother, how they gossiped and played together. The woman unfortunately died in childbirth, and for her sake Titania plans to rear the boy.

How long does she plan to stay in the woods? Oberon wants to know. Perhaps till after Theseus's wedding day, she replies. If the king wants to dance in the moonlight with her, fine; if not, let them be. Oberon wants only the boy. "Not for thy fairy kingdom," cries Titania, and off she goes.

Oberon, a haughty and relentless presence, immediately plots his revenge. He calls Puck to his side, reminiscing about a time he heard a mermaid on a dolphin's back singing so beautifully that "stars shot madly from their spheres" to hear her music. (Scholars have pointed out the similarity between this image and some spectacular court entertainments for Queen Elizabeth in the late sixteenth century. This is sometimes used to help date the writing of *A Midsummer Night's Dream*.) That same time, adds Oberon, he saw Cupid flying, armed with arrows of love. He aimed an arrow at a virgin, but missed. (It has also been suggested that the virgin was a reference to Queen Elizabeth, known as the Virgin Queen.) Oberon, being sharp of eye as well as mind, marked exactly where the misdirected arrow fell. Do you get the feeling this jealous king doesn't miss a thing? He seems to have stored up potential magic charms the way a dog might store some bones. He knows they will come in handy some day.

The arrow fell on a flower, turning it from milkwhite to purple. This startling sexual imagery makes us feel the dangerous and eerie power of Cupid's arrow. The wound it makes is "love's wound." The flower is called love-in-idleness; we know it today as a pansy. Filled with Cupid's magic, this transformed flower has the power to transform others. Its juice, squeezed on a sleeper's eyelids, will make that person fall in love with the next live creature he or she sees. Note Shakespeare's use of the word "creature" to indicate that the love object might not necessarily be human.

NOTE: Shakespeare and flowers: In trying to give you a picture of the power of the fairy world, Shakespeare relies heavily on the use of flowers. They seem to stand as special signposts of magical

transformation. Flowers and plants have traditionally been associated with magic, and in the case of
certain herbs their curative medicinal powers are
well-known. In Shakespeare's time, much scientific, philosophical, and magical investigation was
devoted to the powers and properties of plants
and flowers. But no matter how much scientific
understanding we have of them, their colors and
intricate forms still instill in us a sense of wonder.

Sometimes Shakespeare compares the fairies to
flowers in terms of their height. This makes them
seem as if they're part of another dimension, even
if we can see that on the stage they're the size of
people. Some of the fairies even have floral names,
connecting them to some elemental mystery. Later,
Oberon will repeat the names of flowers as if they
were magical incantations.

Here the love-in-idleness plant is symbolic of the
power in love to change people, altering their inner and outer natures. Swollen as it is with the
"poison" of Cupid's arrow, the flower is the essence of the nature of love. And the nature of love
is at the heart of this play.

Notice also the recurrent theme of eyesight. In
this instance, the eyes of the sleeping lover-to-be
are altered by the juice of the plant. What "creature" this person sees on awakening—worthy or
not—will become the object of love.

Oberon commands Puck to get that flower. The
spriteful Robin obeys quickly: He'll "put a girdle
round about the earth/In forty minutes." Alone,
Oberon tells us his secret plan. Titania is to be the
victim upon whose eyes the charmed juice will work

its magic. And don't expect kindliness from the king; he's not after a prince for his queen. Rather he hopes for something more grotesque: a lion, a bear, a wolf, a bull, or even a monkey. And she won't have her "real" eyes returned until she delivers up the changeling boy to Oberon! How does this nastiness make you feel about Oberon and his potential power? Watch how this edge of danger undercuts the comedy of transformation, keeping dramatic tension alive. With Oberon lurking in the unseen air, how safe would you feel?

Lines 188–268

Approaching voices are heard. Oberon makes himself invisible as Demetrius and Helena enter. They are in the midst of a quarrel. Remember, Helena had told Demetrius of Lysander and Hermia's elopement plan. But he's interested in finding them, not in dealing with Helena. He'll kill the man; the woman is killing him. He commands Helena to go away; he is "wood" (mad) in the wood. But how can Helena go? She is drawn to him as though he were a magnet. If he could stop drawing her, she could stop being drawn. It's a double bind, appropriate to the topsy-turvy, blind nature of love.

Demetrius tells her in the plainest possible terms that he does not and cannot love her. But Helena even loves his honesty in telling her that! She's more than humble at this point—she's humiliated. She'll be his spaniel. He can do whatever he wants with her as long as he does *something* with her.

We're back to opposites in love. Demetrius becomes ill from looking at Helena; Helena becomes ill from not looking at Demetrius. He tries a new tack: she is seriously endangering her precious vir-

ginity by following him in the forest. Helena twists
his words. She is very good at that—her literary
cleverness rarely misses an opportunity to turn a
phrase around. She explains that since he is all the
world to her, she is not really alone with him in
the woods.

Demetrius gives up. All he can think of now is
to run away and leave her at the mercy of wild
beasts. The wildest of those, Helena points out, is
not as heartless as he. The tables will turn, she
warns prophetically. Demetrius tells her once again
to leave him alone, and exits. Helena declares she's
not afraid of any harm to come at his hands; she's
already been hurt. Poor Helena. Her situation is
at once comic and tragic. Her desperate gropings
for love are ridiculous, but painful. The whole reality of romance and the proper relations to it are
being questioned by Shakespeare. Men are supposed to woo women, says Helena, but she finds
herself in the opposite position. The way things
should be and the way they shouldn't change places
in this play. Good and bad, love, life and death
are all mixed up for Helena. "I'll follow thee," she
says, "and make a heaven of hell,/To die upon the
hand I love so well."

Overseeing her predicament, Oberon decides to
intercede. Puck arrives with the magic flower and
gives it to his master. Oberon goes into a dreamy
soliloquy, one of the most beautiful passages in all
of Shakespeare's works, filled with glorious language and an almost sentimental remorse. He describes a favorite place of Titania's. It is a bank
covered in flowers, and the Queen likes to sleep
there, "lulled in these flowers with dances and delight." The snake sheds its skin there, and that

skin is "wide enough to wrap a fairy in." Such delicate details give us more than an idea of the size of the fairy folk; they give us a feeling for the sweet enchantment of their world. But Oberon is not just having a sweet dream. He has a vengeful purpose. If that's where Titania is likely to be, that's where she will be given the magic love juice on her eyes. Oberon also commands Puck to put some juice on the eyes of the Athenian youth he has just seen. He cautions Puck to do it at just the right moment, so that the first thing the young man sees will be the lady who is in love with him. The king would see some things turn out right—or is he just as eager as Puck to turn the world upside down?

NOTE: Titania's resting place   Does the way Shakespeare describes the favorite place of Titania make you want to sleep there yourself, surrounded by its beauty? Shakespeare entices you with great economy of language. The very names of the flowers seem to emit some special power. The thyme blows in the wind, sending its pungent scent around the bank. The violet nods its delicate head. The woodbine ("luscious" makes it seem good to eat as well as to see and smell) forms a canopy over it all, and the musk roses are sweet. To help feel the magic of this passage you might say these words aloud. "Wild thyme," "oxlips," "nodding violet," "luscious woodbine," "sweet musk roses," and "eglantine" roll across the tongue with what seems to be a magic power.

With a leap Puck is off on his mission. He'll be

back before the first rooster can crow. By then, midsummer madness will be in full sway.

ACT II, SCENE II

Lines 1–83

Titania and her loyal group of fairies are in another part of the wood. The queen asks for a ring dance and a song, and then suggests they set about some of their regular fairy business. This includes killing cankers in the musk-rose buds (remember the "sweet musk roses" Oberon spoke of—this must be Titania's favorite resting place!), obtaining bat wings to make coats for her elves, and keeping the hoot owl quiet so it doesn't disturb them. You can see again how these nature-related details used by Shakespeare give us a special awareness of the dimensions of the fairies' world.

The fairies sing a lullaby for their queen. It is a charm that seeks to ward off creepy and crawly things from Titania: snakes, hedgehogs, newts, and worms. They ask for a little musical assistance from Philomele, the nightingale, to lull their lady to sleep. Try to imagine how this chorus of fairies might actually sound. As they repeat their magic syllables—"Lulla, lulla, lullaby, lulla, lulla, lullaby"— feel the sweet drowsiness their birdlike voices induce. Again they warn off some disturbing things: spiders, beetles, worms, and snails. And again the nightingale's sweet song is called for. Shakespeare makes his fairies' natures apparent by the kind (and size) of animals he associates with them. Titania sleeps.

And now it's Oberon's moment. He squeezes the juice from the charmed flower onto Titania's eyelids and requests a different kind of spell. He asks that Titania love whatever she first sees on awakening, and he hopes that will be some "vile thing" like a lynx, cat, bear, leopard, or boar. Again, he reinforces the eyesight theme: "In thy eye that shall appear,/When thou wak'st, it is thy dear." Can you hear Oberon's malicious chuckle as he leaves?

NOTE: The fairies' magic is associated with natural imagery, and like the natural world it can be good or bad, sweet or scary. Titania and her fairies call up the images of small animals and insects. They seem frail (as their potential enemies are small), and their magic spell seeks protection from harm. Oberon, on the other hand, is working a nastier magic. He is causing trouble, not seeking protection from it. Accordingly, the animals he wishes for are more frightening, indicating his more dangerous spell.

Lysander and Hermia enter, exhausted from wandering through the wood. It seems Lysander has lost his way. You can guess that these lovers will be losing more than this particular way. Hermia chooses a soft bank for her bed and suggests Lysander find one for himself. Note that all the while the two are speaking the rhymed poetry of romantic lovers, a courtly and civilized kind of dialogue. But Lysander is suggesting something a little less genteel. He proposes that one "turf" is good enough for both of them. He tries an elaborate sort of poetic seduction. He says that his heart is knit to hers so that they have but one heart and that their lives are pledged together with but one love, so why not share one bed? Hermia agrees his "riddles" are clever, but evades their answer. Modesty decrees they must sleep apart. Hermia here, as usual, retains her feisty independent spirit. The two sleep apart, Lysander pledging eternal loyalty to Hermia and wishing that sleep give her rest. For her part, Hermia wishes Lysander's *eyes* get half that wish for rest. We will see in a moment just what kind of challenge his lover's eyes receive. Note how Shakespeare has utilized his plot devices. Lysander needs to be alone so he can be mistaken by Puck, and Shakespeare creates this comic scene to support it.

Puck arrives, having scoured the forest for the proper Athenian on whom to lay the love charm. He notices Lysander and Hermia, assumes incorrectly they are Demetrius and Helena, and anoints Lysander's eyes with the magic juice. When he wakes, says Puck, there will be no more simple sleep for the eyes of Lysander!

Lines 84–156

As Puck exits, Demetrius and Helena arrive, running. The pace of the plot has picked up now; it's in full farcical swing. Like the Marx brothers or Laurel and Hardy, who go in and out of trick revolving doors in search of each other, these lovers are hot on one another's heels, but always missing each other. A true comedy of errors has begun. Demetrius and Helena are still arguing—one is fleeing, the other pursuing. Finally Demetrius makes his getaway, and Helena is left out of breath.

Helena moans how much better off Hermia is;

the latter's eyes are "blessed and attractive," but they didn't get so bright from being washed with tears. If so, Helena's would be brighter. Helena feels sorry for herself. Everyone (in other words, Demetrius) runs away from her. She must be really ugly. How could she presume to match her eyes with Hermia's? This is Helena's lowest point in the play. She knows the power of the eyes of love and feels she just doesn't have it. In this play of transformations (and split-second timing) what do you think is needed at a character's low point? Of course, a magic charm. Awaking, and rhyming Helena's lament ("Lysander, if you live, good sir, awake"), Lysander leaps up and tells Helena he would "run through fire" for her "sweet sake." For Helena's? Yes. The love juice is working its magic. Lysander is ready simultaneously to love Helena and to kill the vile Demetrius for her sake.

Helena thinks Lysander is angry because Demetrius loves Hermia. She tells him to be content; Hermia still loves him. But that's not the way things are going. It's "not Hermia but Helena I love," vows Lysander. Duped Lysander makes claims for reason. While speaking the most flowery poetry, he says only now reason has led him to Helena's eyes to read the true story of love.

NOTE: Shakespeare really drives home his message. Lysander is completely bewitched by magic, yet claims to be speaking with total reason. How do we know what we know? Have you ever been in, then out of love, and seen with different eyes what you saw before? Shakespeare is telling us there *is* no reason in love. There may be magic in a lover's eyes, but reason? Look again.

Helena feels she is being cruelly mocked and has done nothing to deserve such treatment. It's bad enough to be unloved; does Lysander have to rub it in? She leaves, exasperated. Lysander turns his wandering attentions to the sleeping Hermia. He is sick of her sweetness and ashamed of having been duped by her. From now on, all the love and honor of this noble knight will be directed toward Helena. He leaves to pursue her. Shakespeare's mockery of heroic illusion rubs Lysander's eyes and tongue in the mud. This is a lover truly lost in love.

Hermia awakes from a bad dream, screaming for Lysander to help her. She has dreamed a serpent was eating her heart while Lysander smiled. She goes in search of either death or her false lover.

ACT III

ACT III, SCENE I

Lines 1–114
As Titania lies asleep nearby on her bank of flowers, the workingmen arrive in the wood to rehearse "Pyramus and Thisby." Quince finds the spot suitable enough, and they plan to enact the play just as they will perform it later before the duke. But first Bottom has a question: If in this comedy Pyramus must draw a sword and kill himself, wouldn't that unnecessarily scare the women?

Snout and Starveling agree; maybe it would be better to leave the killing out. But Bottom has a better plan. Why not write a prologue that explains that the sword is not real, that Pyramus is not really dead, and, what's more, that Pyramus is actually Bottom the weaver! Bottom's plans always enlarge the role for himself. Though he seems to have the welfare of the whole company in mind, he's always looking out for some special effect for himself.

NOTE: Theatrical conventions Remember how the theater itself is connected to the tension between illusion and reality? It's funny to think Bottom might be worried about people's believing that he (as Pyramus) is really dead. The conventions of theater make it easy for us to believe in some things and not in others. But the interplay is very subtle. In some way we "believe" in Bottom, that these words and thoughts are his. And yet, keeping in mind that, ideally, we'd be watching the play performed, we know the words would actually be spoken by an actor who certainly is *not* Bottom. And even beyond that, the words are actually Shakespeare's. While we may laugh at Bottom for thinking the audience takes his killing as real, Shakespeare slyly laughs at us for taking his character Bottom as real. A great artist makes us believe in his characters and events. An even greater artist can show us his conventions—the strings that hold up the puppet—and still make us believe, laughing at the power of our imaginations. Watch how this tension is heightened by challenging other conventions. What element of theater, for instance, might the discussion of the man in the moon and his lantern be pointing to?

Quince agrees to the prologue. Then Snout brings up the problem of the lion: mightn't it be too frightening as well? Bottom agrees, characteristically showing off his ignorance with a verbal flourish, calling the lion a "fearful wild fowl." Foul he may be, but fowl, no. (Scholars often use the somewhat similar appearance of a lion before an Elizabethan court performance to help date this play.) Bottom really gets into it now, making sure no spectator will miss the difference between theatrical illusion and reality. He suggests that the lion wear only a partial mask and give a short explanation to the audience (Bottom offers four different ways to begin this short apology, resourceful as always) that reveals the lion to be none other than an actor—Snug, to be precise. Can you feel Shakespeare's tease? He's really stretching the limit of what we might believe "before our eyes." Quince nicely agrees to that suggestion too and adds a problem of his own. What will they do about moonlight, which shines when Pyramus and Thisby meet? Consulting a calendar, the rustics find that the real moon will be shining the night of the performance. If they leave a casement window open, it will shine for their play. Then the real moon will also be the theatrical moon. Bottom suggests a person might play the man in the moon, with his legendary Elizabethan properties (firewood and a lantern). And since Pyramus and Thisby converse through a chink in a wall, they'll need someone to represent a wall, too. You can see how far this absurd play between illusion and reality could go. All that taken care of, they begin to rehearse.

Suddenly Puck appears. He can't resist playing with the players. Bottom begins his flowery speech, using the word "odious" instead of "odors," then exits. Thisby (Flute) hesitatingly begins his poetic call to Pyramus, a ridiculous, confused bit of poetic language. Like the contradictory "lamentable comedy," Pyramus is described as both "lily-white of hue" and colored "like the red rose." Like Bottom, Flute also mispronounces a word. (*Ninus's* tomb— Ninus was a legendary hero, founder of the Biblical city Nineveh—becomes *Ninny's* tomb.) In addition, he's jumped his cue: he's added the wrong line at the wrong time. When he repeats the correct cue line, Bottom appears, sporting an ass's head the mischievous Puck has placed on him. The company flees in terror. Puck swears to follow them around the forest, appearing in the forms of various animals. He knows he has them scared at night in the woods and is going to have some fun. Bottom's reply is touching: "Why do they run away?" He's left alone, transfigured but unaware of it.

NOTE: Now all the interplay between illusion and reality, and the metamorphosis from one to the other, begins to compound. The fairy magic moves from realm to realm. The themes of illusion in love and illusion in the theater begin to interweave. And in case we were taking comfort that the character Bottom at least was real, he too is changed. Is he really an ass, or does he just appear that way in one light? In another light, especially to Titania, he will appear differently, indeed. Bottom seems to act like an ass at times. Yet his simple, well-meaning ignorance in a way makes him lovable; he's really not such an ass. If you feel that way—and Shakespeare surely leads us toward that sympathetic feeling—how far are your eyes from Titania's? Shakespeare's comedy mercilessly attacks all the conventions by which we measure and establish someone's beauty and lovability.

Lines 115–201
Snout reappears. "O Bottom," he says, "thou art changed! What do I see on thee?" Bottom replies that it's an ass head of Snout's own, again pointing to the responsibility in the seer for what he's seeing. Bottom, of course, doesn't know what his *own* head looks like. Quince takes another look and flees again. Bottom thinks he sees their jest; they are making fun of him. (Helena has this same feeling when love is turned her way.) But he won't fall for their trick and get scared. He'll hold his ground and sing to pass the time.

He sings a little nature tune about birds, and you can imagine what Bottom might sound like singing a sweet little folk melody, and how he'd look with his new head. But to Titania, awaking from sleep, there is nothing silly about it. "What angel wakes me from my flow'ry bed?" is her classic question. Angel? Looking at Bottom and hearing that word, suddenly we know the terrible and ridiculous power of Cupid's dart. How easily our eyes can be fooled!

Bottom breaks off his song, questioning the meaning of a line. Titania, entranced with the music, begs him to continue. She's in a dreamy, swoony delight. See how our very language fools us—she's awake, but her mind's eye is still dreaming. And that same "eye" is "enthralled" by the sight of Bottom, enough so that—on first sight—she must say to him, "I love thee." It's the kind of remark that should make anyone who's ever been in love wince. If you could see yourself as others see you, how would you look with your arms entwined around an ass?

Bottom takes her declaration in stride, questioning the aptness of that statement. "And yet," he adds, "to say the truth, reason and love keep little company together nowadays."

Remember, Lysander claimed to be speaking out of reason when he proclaimed his charmed love for Helena. Bottom's statement couldn't be more basic to the play.

But such reasoning doesn't unhook Titania; it drives her into deeper trouble. In fact, it makes Bottom seem "deep" to her. Now she thinks he is wise, not just beautiful. She wants him to stay with her. Queenlike, she commands him, though it's also the command of seduction. She will give him fairies to attend to his needs. They'll bring him jewels and sing to him while he sleeps on a bed of flowers, and she will give his mortal body the lightness of a spirit. She calls four fairies and instructs them in their fairy duties with characteristic Shakespearean detail, the kind of minute and magical descriptions that make us believe—or want to believe—that a fairy world might be real. They'll feed him little fruits and berries, steal honey bags from the bees, and "pluck the wings from painted butterflies/To fan the moonbeams from his sleeping eyes." Noticing these tiny things opens up a new perspective on the world for us, and through that opening Shakespeare lets his fairies flit through.

Peaseblossom, Cobweb, Moth, and Mustard-seed salute Bottom. He rather gallantly speaks to each in turn, joking with them and enjoying his pampered part. The goodness of Bottom's heart shows through his respectful treatment of the fairies. Although probably large and certainly gross with his ass's head, he is gentle—even genteel—with the delicate fairies. Bottom, who as his name implies is as down-to-earth as could be, also possesses the ability to reach across into this other realm. His is the one human voyage that explores all the levels of Shakespeare's meaning in the play: love, theater, and magic. Other characters are affected by the fairies' charms, but Bottom is actually involved in their ethereal world. Is he gross, is he ugly, is he a bore? Maybe so. But see how Bottom's reactions with the fairies make your feelings about him more complex.

Titania is impatient with love. The moon (at every turn we are reminded of the moon) seems to be weeping for some violation of chastity. Is this grotesque romance about to be consummated? Titania has her conquest. She's not too much bewitched by love, though, to notice that Bottom can get awfully long-winded. "Tie up my lover's tongue," she commands; "bring him silently."

ACT III, SCENE II

Lines 1–121

Oberon encounters Puck in another part of the woods. The king wonders if his plans of vengeance for Titania have taken place. Puck's ecstatic answer meets all of Oberon's "vilest" wishes: "My mistress with a monster is in love." Puck gleefully recounts his mischief with the troupe of actors.

You can almost see him acting out the entire scene as he tells it to Oberon, laughing all the while. He explains how Bottom's appearance with the ass's head exploded their calm rehearsal, as the actors flew away like birds hearing a gunshot. In their confusion and fear they ran through the woods, with both Puck and the briars plucking at their clothing. We know the punchline: "Titania waked, and straightway loved an ass."

Oberon agrees this turned out better than expected. But how about the Athenian? he wants to know. Puck tells him that has also been taken care of. As if to prove the point, Hermia and Demetrius enter. This plot, so ripe with perfect timing and coincidences, sometimes seems magical itself. Oberon and Puck discover the mistake.

NOTE: Just as you learn from your own mistakes, see what you can learn from the "mistakes" in the play. Imagine what the play would have been like if Hermia and Lysander loved each other and if Helena and Demetrius loved each other, in simple order. Then look what happens because of the mix-ups. See how the twists of fate reveal Shakespeare's meaning about the nature of love.

Demetrius, as usual, is doting on Hermia. She, as usual, is fed up with him. But this time she has the added suspicion that he has killed Lysander while she slept. Hermia is still sure of Lysander's devotion. She couldn't possibly imagine the trick that's about to be revealed to her. To her, Lysander's love is truer than the sun is to the day. Since you have already heard how Oberon and Titania's quarrel has upset the order of the natural world, you may realize Hermia's comparison is not as stable as it might first seem. But Hermia can't believe Lysander would have stolen away from her, and she piles up more images of natural harmony to prove her case to Demetrius.

Demetrius would rather speak love poetry than answer the accusation. He feels murdered by Hermia's cruelty. Hermia has no patience for his extravagant phrases. Where, she wants to know, is her Lysander? Will he give him to her? Demetrius responds coldly that he'd rather give the carcass to his hounds. This really works up Hermia to a point of agitation. You can feel the threat of physical violence in her mood. He, she says, is the dog. She insists on the truth: Has he killed Lysander while he slept? Demetrius replies he has neither seen nor killed Lysander. His tone tells us he'd rather be talking about other things with Hermia. Since he can't give her the information she seeks, Hermia leaves in a huff, hoping to see Demetrius no more. He, for his part, is thoroughly worn out. Sorrow, he says, is made heavier in him by his lack of sleep. To ease it, he lies down and sleeps.

Oberon admonishes Puck for his mistake. Because of it, a true love has been turned, "and not a false turned true." Puck replies that those are the rules of fate. For every man holding true in love, a million fail, breaking their oaths again and again. This twist is not exactly what Oberon had in mind. He was hoping to remedy a situation, not make it worse. Though he is angry at Titania, he does have some sympathy for love. He instructs Puck to find Helena and bring her to him. Puck flies off like an arrow. Oberon, holding the purple flower swollen with the wound from Cupid's dart, drops the magic juice on the eyelids of sleeping Demetrius. When he sees Helena, she will shine like Venus, the evening star. In a twinkle Puck returns. He has with him not just Helena but Lysander, too. Puck never chooses the simple route. He'll always try to throw something extra into the bargain. He likes these complications. They're entertainment to him. "Lord," he exclaims, "what fools these mortals be!" He knows what will happen when Demetrius wakes up. Two will woo one, and that will be sport for Puck. He admits it: he is best pleased by those things that turn preposterous. Is that unfair? Is Puck just a troublemaker, or do his manipulations reveal us to ourselves?

NOTE: Truth and falseness now are spelled out as themes in the play. Did you think love was always "True Love"? Puck makes it clear the odds are very different. The odds on true love versus false love are a million to one. It becomes clear that humans are going to need very special, accurate eyes to be able to see love clearly. Puck's mischief turns a supposedly true love inside out. Maybe Lysander's love was that one-in-a-million. But after seeing the ease with which the potion changes lovers' feelings, don't you begin to wonder if they might be a little changeable anyway—even without the juice? In what ways are human lovers fools, or in what ways is Puck just making fools of them?

Lines 122–277
Lysander is defending himself against Helena's accusations. He shows off his tears as badges of his

true feeling. Twice he mentions truth, which must ring as hollowly in our ears at this point as it does in Helena's. She says his truths kill each other. The vows weigh nothing; they're empty if he deals them equally to Hermia and herself. Lysander says his vows to Hermia lacked judgment—a clear picture of the value of a lover's judging ability! Helena replies he's really lacking judgment if he gives Hermia up. Lysander tries another tack. Demetrius, he insists, loves Hermia, not Helena. Could there be a better cue? Demetrius, awakening, leaps to his feet, calls Helena a goddess, and spouts an outlandish set of swoony, ecstatic, romantic lines. This language begins to mock not just love but Elizabethan love poetry, too. In fact, it sounds like a takeoff on one of Shakespeare's own sonnets: "Shall I compare thee to a summer's day," for instance. Demetrius is full tilt into his romantic rhetoric, going first for the eyes (not surprisingly, given what we've seen about the importance of eyes in the play), then the cherry lips, then Helena's white hand. Love poetry has rarely sounded so hollow. Who could trust someone spouting phrases like that? Lack of trust, of course, goes hand in hand with lack of truth.

Helena sees the mockery, but thinks both men are part of a plot to make fun of her. Couldn't they just hate her, she asks, instead of mocking her? She's weepy and pouty and very perturbed, knowing they both love Hermia.

Not liking to see their "true love" so upset, the two men let fly with accusations. Lysander offers a pretty little speech, yielding up Hermia to Demetrius and accepting Helena in exchange. Demetrius is not interested. If he ever did love Hermia, it was just temporary. Now his heart has returned home to Helena. But here, he adds, as Hermia enters, is Lysander's dear love.

Though the night has clouded her sight, Hermia's "ear" has helped her find Lysander. Why, she wants to know, did he leave her?

NOTE: Hermia remains constant in her love for Lysander (as does Helena in her love for Demetrius). Her eyes see truly, not falsely. But in this magic, changeable moonlight, her eyesight isn't able to penetrate the dark. Her "true" Lysander isn't really there to be seen.

Lysander instantly shows his changed mood. Love made him go—love for fair Helena. In fact, after some flowery building up of Helena's beauty, he declares he hates Hermia. She, of course, is astonished. So is Helena. She now thinks all three are out to make fun of her. She chides Hermia. Is this what comes from all their days of friendship, when they embroidered and sang as if they were one person? Like a double cherry or berry, they grew together. Will Hermia cut apart their friendship now with her mockery?

Hermia, of course, doesn't know what Helena's talking about. She feels scorned herself. Helena asks if Hermia didn't put Lysander and Demetrius up to all that puffy poetry. It has to be through Hermia's goading. Though Hermia continues to protest, Helena is too wound up to stop. She's so used to being unloved she knows there has to be some trickery behind this new situation. (Unfortunately, she doesn't know the right mischief maker to suspect.) Paranoid, she projects her insecurity onto all of them, imagining winks and laughs behind her back. She'll leave rather than endure this mockery. If you've ever been in a situation where you imagine there is a conspiracy against you, you may realize what pain Helena is in.

Lysander tries poetry again. Hermia, still lovingly faithful to Lysander, herself begins to think he's making fun of Helena. Then the two men have a contest of vows, each protesting his love for Helena. Words fly back and forth. The men are ready to fight it out. Hermia tries to hold Lysander back, and he lets loose a startling run of rude remarks to her. She is an "Ethiope," a "cat," a "burr," a "vile thing," a "tawny Tartar." These remarks are hitting below the belt. Her dark beauty is now cruelly devalued, and Hermia begins to see that Lysander is not joking. Though Lysander wants to fight Demetrius, he can't hurt Hermia to make her let him go—even though he hates her.

That's the final blow to Hermia. What harm, she asks, could be worse than his hate? She doesn't understand what's happened. "Am not I Hermia? Are not you Lysander?" She's the same woman she was, but "since night you loved me; yet since night you left me." If she's the same, then Lysander must indeed be different.

Hermia's question is right to the point. Is he or is he not Lysander? Isn't the character of a lover measured by his love? How do Lysander's actions make you feel about him and Hermia? Can you hold someone accountable who has been charmed by Cupid's dart? Notice, too, how the implied danger keeps a dark current of satire running through the comic farce.

Lines 278–400

Lysander puts it plainly. He's not jesting. He hates
Hermia and loves Helena. Now Hermia turns to
her rival. Her temper is up and she thinks now
that she's the one being made a fool of. Helena,
she says, is a "thief of love." The confusion works
both women up to a fever. Helena still thinks she's
being mocked. Hermia, she says, is a puppet, a
counterfeit. Hermia takes this as another slur on
her physical nature—she's small. She thinks Helena must have used her height to gain the attention of Lysander. You can see the argument's be-
coming laughable as each woman projects her
confusion and insecurity onto the other. Hermia,
formerly so sweet and steadfast in her love, becomes something of a terror. It seems in anger these
women reveal more of their character than when
they're holding to love. While the men project the
same sappy romantic lyricism, the women battle it
out.

Hermia throws back the slurs at Helena, the
"painted maypole." She's ready to scratch out her
eyes. Helena, taken aback, appeals to the men for
protection. Nevertheless, she slyly lets loose another arrow, again mentioning Hermia's "lower"
stature. But really Helena just wants out of the
situation. She can't quite understand what's gone
on. She refers to her fond and simple nature. She
just loves Demetrius as always. She's been true to
Hermia, she explains, and merely followed Demetrius into the woods. It's foolishness, not cunning, that got her there. And even though she wants
to go, her loving heart keeps her there with Demetrius.

The men take Helena's part, offering to protect

her. Again the slurs fly, with Lysander's comments to Hermia rudest of all. If he is flowery in love, he is downright dirty in disaffection. Even Demetrius is shocked. With Hermia temporarily knocked out by rudeness, the men are free to fight. They exit with fists raised.

Now the women are left alone. Hermia turns in anger toward Helena, but Helena takes advantage of her longer legs and runs away. Hermia, dazed by it all, leaves as well.

Oberon and Puck have been watching the confusion. Oberon puts the blame on Puck. He either made a mistake or acted willfully. Puck protests his innocence. He was merely told of "the Athenian"; it really wasn't his fault. He's not sorry though, since he's gotten some entertainment from his mistake. We know that's what he likes best. But Oberon has more compassion. He's a king, remember, and a powerful spirit. He doesn't want the men to hurt each other. He explains in detail a further mission for Puck: he's to spread a thick fog over the two lovers. Then Puck is to lead them around, faking his voice first as Lysander, then as Demetrius, thoroughly confusing them, and tiring them out.

NOTE: Oberon's speech befits his royal power. In contrast to that of the lovers, his poetry rings with grandeur and truth. It lends his thoughts a knowledge that seems more than mortal. He *does* have eyes that can see beyond the blindness of love, and he will work the lovers toward a true love's end.

Oberon instructs Puck to once again apply a magic juice to Lysander's eyes, this time from the flower that has the ability to release the Cupid charm, returning Lysander to his original devotion. "When they next wake," he says, "all this derision/Shall seem a dream and fruitless vision." You begin to see how the power of love is likened to the power of dream. Midsummer madness clouds sight. True love's eyes are needed to see through its "dream."

This business taken care of, Oberon will tend to his queen. He'll once again ask Titania for the changeling, then release her from her spell. Puck warns that this must be done fast. The charmed night is ending, and the ghosts and "damned spirits" will be returning to their proper haunts, ashamed to be seen in daylight. Oberon agrees, but explains "we are spirits of another sort." He has frequently made love to the Morning spirit. He's not afraid of daylight. He often confronts the dawn, glorying in the "blessed beams" of the sun as it turns the ocean gold. Even so, he agrees they must act fast. Bouncing up and down, Puck takes off to remedy the situation.

NOTE: Oberon makes clear that he and his fairy folk are essentially good spirits. They're not demons like other night creatures. We have seen they are powerful; now Shakespeare shows us that their power works ultimately for the resolution of love. Again you can measure Oberon by the power of his poetry. His description of the sunrise is itself beautiful magic. There's no better way to feel the spirit of the fairies than to let yourself experience Oberon's charmed language.

Lines 401–463

Lysander stumbles back onto the scene, chasing his phantom Demetrius. As he exits, Demetrius enters, lured by Puck's imitations. Puck plays with him mercilessly, goading him onward. When Demetrius leaves, Lysander returns. He can't figure out what's going on. Every time Demetrius calls, Lysander follows—only to find no one there. Tired and confused, he lies down to sleep. Once more Demetrius is lured back, with Puck running circles around him. Demetrius is worn out from the mockery. He's just an angry lover who wants to fight but can't seem to find the enemy. Faint and weary, he too lies down to sleep.

If there is to be reunion from this confusion, everybody must be assembled. Sure enough, Helena wanders into sight. It's been a long night. She appeals to the dawn to come so that she can return to Athens, and looks toward sleep to deliver her from her heavy sorrows. Did she just happen to appear? No, Puck is behind it all, counting bodies. Only three? Two couples need four lovers: here's the last. Hermia drags herself in, "Bedabbled with the dew and torn with briars." Her legs can't move anymore. With the true sweetness and devotion of her character, she prays that Lysander be protected if he and Demetrius really do fight.

As the lovers sleep, Puck speaks his magic rhymes. He anoints Lysander's eyes with the redeeming juice: "True delight" in Hermia will re-

turn to him. Puck promises order will be restored.
"Jack shall have Jill," just as the story says, ". . .
and all shall be well."

NOTE: The frantic comedy of the lovers draws
to a close. The farce is worked up to a fever pitch,
with entrances and exits made so fast you can hardly
keep track of them. But as you laugh at the mix-
ups of these poor bedraggled lovers, notice how
Shakespeare is able to raise real questions about
truth and love, right in the midst of your laughter.

ACT IV

ACT IV, SCENE I

Lines 1–104

Titania now enters the scene with her fairies and
Bottom in tow. Oberon follows, unseen by them.
Titania asks Bottom to sit beside her so she may
stroke his cheeks, place musk roses on his head,
and kiss his "fair large ears." Her eyes are still
charmed, and Bottom's ass's ears are beautiful
things to her. Bottom is enjoying all the attention.
His transformed nature seems to have made him
a bit lethargic—maybe the new head is too heavy
for him. He asks Peaseblossom to scratch it. Cobweb's services are also required; he is to bring Bottom a honey bag from the top of a thistle, being
careful that it doesn't break. True to his current
kingly position, Bottom cares about his new subjects; he doesn't want the honey to spill all over
Cobweb. Some genuine kindness always seems to

come through him, even in his most preposterous situations.

Next Bottom calls to Mustardseed to help with the scratching. The humor comes from Bottom's innocence about how he looks. He marvels at his itchy hairiness as if it were just an overgrown beard. And if he itches, he must scratch. Titania, still doting in love, asks if Bottom would like to hear some music. She probably has in mind some ethereal fairy music. Bottom, true to his workingman's nature, calls for the "tongs and the bones"—metal and bone clappers used by the poorer classes. You can see how Shakespeare always tries to heighten the ridiculousness of the situation by pointing out with details the differences between Bottom's and Titania's natural worlds. It makes their relationship even more absurd. They remain blissfully ignorant of a situation that is perfectly obvious to us. Have you ever wondered how someone in love can "see" what he or she does in another person? Titania swooning over ass-headed Bottom highlights just that predicament. What would her sweet like to eat? Oh, some "good dry oats" or a bundle of "sweet hay" would suit him just fine. Titania says her fairy shall seek him out some nuts. Bottom responds that some dried peas sound more like it. But in truth he needs to sleep. That's fine for Titania. She'll wind her arms around him just as the ivy twists around the elm. (Plant life, again, is the appropriate image for fairy magic.) She loves Bottom—she "dotes" on him.

NOTE: "Doting" is Shakespeare's code word for love under the spell of romantic illusion, love that is, in fact, blind. In Act I, Scene I, Lysander, describing Demetrius's unworthiness, mentions how Helena cannot see this. Instead, she "dotes,/ Devoutly dotes, dotes in idolatry" on him. She doesn't see his character. She only sees what her eyes want her to see. The same is true for Titania. This time the illusory mechanism of love is highlighted by the use of the love juice to turn Titania's eyes from true to false sight.

Puck enters and Oberon welcomes him. Oberon says he is beginning to pity Titania's doting on Bottom. He may also be a little jealous. He recently ran into her winding flowers in Bottom's hair, and the sight was too much for him.

Notice how Oberon always has a command of poetry, even when he is merely describing an event. First he describes the dew that normally lies on flower buds as round and lustrous pearls. But since that image is not appropriate to the current situation, he changes "pearls" to "tears," thus reflecting his sadness about his and Titania's quarrel and separation.

While Oberon was taunting Titania, and while she was thoroughly distracted with her new love, he asked again for the changeling boy, and this time Titania gave him to Oberon. Now that the king has gotten what he wanted he is ready to undo the charm from his queen's eyes. He also instructs Puck to remove the ass's head from Bottom. When Bottom awakens, he will "think no more of this night's accidents/ But as the fierce vexation of a dream." But first, with another rhyming spell, he removes the charm of Cupid's flower with the remedy of "Dian's bud."

NOTE: Diana, moon goddess, was the protector of virgins. Thus it is mythically appropriate to have her flower counteract the magic of Cupid's all-too-ready passion.

Notice, also, how Oberon brings the theme of "dreaming" into the play. Sleeping/dreaming now takes on the same kind of opposition as reality/illusion and truth/falsehood have had. The characters will all begin to awaken from their "Midsummer Night's Dream" into their true, natural "seeing." Think about how dreaming relates to the major themes of the play. How is love like a dream? How is the spectacle of theater like dream images?

Titania awakes as if from a vision. In her dream she thought she was in love with an ass. Oberon points to the very ass in question. Now Titania's eyes loathe the sight of him. Oberon instructs Puck to remove the charmed head from Bottom and calls for music. Puck says now Bottom will see with his "own fool's eyes." Oberon and Titania dance and Oberon celebrates the return of love by pledging that they will dance again the next night to honor the wedding of Theseus and Hippolyta. Then, too, the other lovers will be blessed in marriage. As Puck remarks the lark's announcement of morning, Titania and Oberon leave together. She asks that he explain the night's strange proceedings. How much of the story do you think Oberon will tell her?

Lines 105–222
Theseus and Hippolyta enter, with Egeus and their train of attendants. They have been observing the rites of May (such as Lysander mentioned in Act

I, Scene I, line 167), and now, since it's still early, Theseus wants Hippolyta to hear the music his hunting hounds make as they bark.

The abrupt difference between Theseus's hunting music and the music we just heard in fairyland is telling. Now it is morning; the magical moonlit night of the play's title is over. Theseus's hounds trumpet a return to reality, to social order as opposed to madness, and to marriage as opposed to passionate doting.

Hippolyta mentions that once when she was in Crete with Hercules and Cadmus she heard Spartan hounds as they cornered a bear. The entire surroundings seemed to resound with the barking, like thunder. Theseus notes his hounds are bred from the Spartan kind; they have the same sandy color, hanging cheeks, and long ears. Though they are slow, their voices are matched like bells.

NOTE: Elizabethan hounds Though it sounds strange to us, in Elizabethan times the music of hunting hounds was well prized. Often, different kinds and sizes of dogs were chosen for a pack in order to create a kind of barking harmony.

But before Theseus can sound off the dogs for Hippolyta, he sees something. This spot, of course, is still the same place where the lovers and Bottom all fell asleep—and they are still there sleeping. Egeus, Hermia's father, at once recognizes his daughter, her two suitors, and Helena. Though Egeus wonders what they might be doing there, Theseus charitably supposes they had gotten up early to perform the rites of May and pay homage to the duke and his bride-to-be. Then he remembers: Isn't this the day Hermia was to have given her answer about her choice, to live with Demetrius, die, or join a nunnery? Egeus nods; Theseus commands the huntsmen to sound their horns. Once again people are waking up. But now the enchanted night is over; the solemnities of approaching marriage are enforcing reality.

Theseus greets the lovers with a bawdy remark about birds mating on St. Valentine's day. Then he sizes up the situation. He knows Demetrius and Lysander are bitter rivals. Then why are they sleeping near each other without thought of their safety? Lysander, amazed, half asleep and half awake, tries to piece the puzzle together for Theseus. All that we have seen transpire is but a foggy dream to Lysander now. He can't even remember it, though he seems to know he's been through something. Going back to the beginning, he explains his and Hermia's plans for escape. Egeus is outraged and calls for the law to be enforced. He explains to Demetrius that Lysander would have stolen Hermia from him.

This Demetrius knows through Helena, though he too is disoriented from the midsummer dream. Remembering, he describes how he trailed Hermia and Lysander into the woods, with Helena following him. He doesn't know how, but somehow his love for Hermia has melted like snow and seems like a memory of some childhood fascination with a trinket that he used to "dote" upon. Now, his heart is focused on Helena, whom he was engaged to before he first saw Hermia. His love for Hermia was like a sickness; now he has come back to his "natural taste." Demetrius has been doubly charmed. First he loved Helena; then Hermia charmed his eyes; then Oberon charmed his eyes back to Helena. What's "natural" in this affection is hard, indeed, to tell!

Theseus finds that things have turned out rather neatly. He overrules Egeus and declares the two couples will be married at the same time as he and Hippolyta. Theseus, as the representative of social and political order, legislates the final harmony of love and matrimony for Hermia and Lysander, Helena and Demetrius. This done, the duke and his courtiers return to Athens.

The lovers are still in a bit of a stupor. Demetrius can't quite make out what's gone on. The happenings are like a far-off vista where mountains melt into clouds. To Hermia everything is slightly out of focus, as if he has double vision. Demetrius puts it succinctly: "Are you sure/That we are awake?" he asks. "It seems to me/That yet we sleep, we dream." Shakespeare doesn't let us completely off the hook. Though for now things are resolved in marriage, the nature of love will remain as perplexing as ever. How did these revelations make you feel about the lovers? What level of trust do you have in them now? They all agree, at least, that the duke was there. Therefore, they must be awake. They too resolve to return to Athens, recounting their dreams along the way.

Bottom is left to rouse himself. He awakens as if he were still in the middle of rehearsing "Pyramus and Thisby"—the very point at which he was "transformed" by Puck. He calls to his fellow actors, thinking they must have stolen away while he slept. Then he remembers . . . well, he half remembers. But Bottom didn't have just a dream; he had a "vision." And it seems to him beyond the ability of man to say what his dream was. Man would be an "ass" to try to recount it. He tries— but no, he can't reach it. It's beyond his mortal grasp. He's back to characteristic form, his senses and words all jumbled. His eyes can't hear and his ears can't see well enough to recount the dream. His hand can't taste it, his tongue can't conceive it, and his heart can't speak about it. He resolves to have Quince write a "ballet" (he means "ballad") about it. It will be called "Bottom's Dream" because it has no bottom. The actor in him revives: he'll sing the ballad at the end of the play to entertain the duke!

NOTE: Bottom's dream   Unlike the lovers, Bottom had actual connections to the fairy world and seems also to be more deeply connected to his dream than anyone else. He, alone, recognizes its visionary nature. He was, after all, literally transformed by his experience, and some of that transformation remains. For all his foolishness and arrogance, Bottom is able to hold onto some of the magic that transpired. Though he isn't smart enough to fathom it all, he isn't stupid enough to discount it as a mere dream. Man, he seems to say, must be willing to rest in some kind of mystery. In a way this is like the Christian doctrine of faith: people cannot know God's mind and will, and so must rely on faith. Bottom has a kind of purity of faith. The humor is still there: his mix-up of the senses is a take-off on a passage from I Corinthians about man's inability to understand God's will. But something innocent and reverent shines through the humor. His amazed state keeps things alive, keeps them in question. He won't let there be a final resolution between dreaming and being awake. There is still some fairy dust on his head.

ACT IV, SCENE II

Back in Quince's house in Athens the would-be actors are in distress. Where is their star, Bottom? Starveling suggests he must have been "transported"—carried off by the fairies. This joke, we know, is all too true. If he doesn't come, Flute wants to know, can the play still be performed? Quince says there's not another man in Athens able to play Pyramus. Flute glumly agrees: Bottom is the wittiest of the workingmen in town. Quince notes Bottom is also the handsomest and a "very paramour for a sweet voice." He meant to say "paragon," as Flute points out. A "paramour" is a worthless man. (After what we've seen of paramours in the preceding acts, Flute clearly has a point.)

Snug enters with even more upsetting news. It turns out there will be several weddings, not just the duke's. If they'd been able to perform, adds Flute, they'd have been given sixpence a day for life by the duke.

Before things get too gloomy, Bottom strides in, calling for his "lads," his "hearts." It's clear from both their previous distress and his affectionate terminology that these men have great feeling for each other. Their comradely manner, easy and spontaneous, is in great contrast to the courtly and complex relations of the lovers. Quince expresses his delight in seeing Bottom. Bottom, still somewhat transfixed from his vision, promises to give a discourse on the wonders that have befallen him. Then he changes his mind; then again swears to tell all. Why do you think he has trouble describing his dream? Put yourself in Bottom's shoes. How much would you want to tell of your transformation? And if you tried, would you be able to find the words to describe it?

Now Bottom takes charge of the troupe. Their play has been chosen. He has his crew gather their motley properties. With good strings on their beards, new ribbons on their shoes, clean linen for Thisby, and unclipped nails for the lion, they should be able to work some good effects. One more thing, says Bottom: don't eat onions or garlic: sweet breath will produce sweet comedy. You've heard Bottom do a bombastic speech before, with its hard-pressed alliterations. You can see why he makes this final admonition. The troupe leaves to prepare the performance of their "lamentable comedy."

ACT V

ACT V, SCENE I

Lines 1–107
In the palace of the duke, Theseus, Hippolyta, Philostrate, and the royal court assemble to begin the wedding festivities. Having heard the lovers speak of their adventures, Hippolyta admits their tales sound a little strange, but she half believes them. Theseus, ever the rational man, thinks their stories more strange than true. They're just fairy tales to

him, and you can see how his rational mind blocks out even the possibility that fairies are real. Theseus says that lovers and madmen create fantasies in their overheated minds that are way beyond what reasonable minds can comprehend. In fact, he adds, the lunatic, the lover, and the poet are similar. The first sees more devils than there are in hell. The second looks at the face of a gypsy and sees there the great mythic beauty Helen. And the poet looks all around him, and as his imagination busies itself with phantom forms, his pen gives them shape and substance. He says that imagination is able to perform these tricks: if it wants some joy, it creates a bringer of that joy; if it perceives some fear, then it can turn a bush into a bear.

NOTE: This speech of Theseus is one of the most famous passages in the play. In it Shakespeare shows the power of the mind to deceive itself, but also to engage in true creation. There are two sides to the mind's dialogue with illusion and reality. You have seen how the lovers' false sight can lead them astray into "doting." But clearly Shakespeare's own art, that of the "poet," is able, by its shape-creating, to bring you to deeper values and understandings of human nature.

Readers have also seen Theseus in two ways. Some feel his speech indicates an inability to see things outside the realm of reason, like true passion or art. Others feel that Theseus is a ruler exercising the caution proper to his office, but that his speech about the poet indicates a real sympathy for the magical workings of art. Which side are you on? Watch the way Theseus responds to the announcement of the workingmen's entertainment for a clue to his feelings toward art.

The lovers enter and salute the duke. Theseus inquires what entertainments have been scheduled to while away the time before the newlyweds can go to bed. He is, just as at the beginning, the impatient lover—three hours are a torturous "long age" to him. Philostrate, the master of the revels, presents him with a choice of plays. Theseus reads through the list. It's really a ridiculous array of the stock, corny, and inappropriate theatricals common to Elizabethan entertainments, though Shakespeare seems to be pushing it far toward the improbable in his satire. A battle of the centaurs to be sung by a eunuch doesn't sound quite right for a pre-wedding-night ceremony. Nor does a presentation of the Bacchanals, devotees of the god Dionysus, who in their drunken frenzy ripped people to pieces. The Muses mourning "for the death/Of Learning" is certainly inappropriate and tedious sounding. In this company, "Pyramus and Thisby" stands out as a possible goof, if nothing else. Theseus immediately gets the irony (though unintended) of the combination "tragical mirth." Though Philostrate tries to dissuade him (having seen the rehearsal), Theseus chooses the "lamentable comedy." Even if, as Philostrate says, the company has no skill in acting, Theseus is willing to hear them out. He believes that their simple earnestness will be enough to justify their art. Hippolyta, though, is anxious. She doesn't like to see people embarass themselves by attempting more than they are capable of.

Again you can see the dual nature of Theseus.

He may not have much understanding of the artistic process, but he has respect for people—his subjects—and their attempts at fulfilling their duties to him. He's used to seeing people stumble and stutter in his presence. He's enough of a statesman to understand that intentions are what matter. He's even had scholars greet him, getting their punctuation all confused and putting periods in the middle of sentences. Which is right to the point, because here comes nervous Quince doing just that in his bumbling prologue to the play.

Lines 108–218

Quince sets forth a puzzle, and you can play with it to unravel it and make sense. He is so discombobulated that he stops and starts in all the wrong places. It's just a simple prologue about coming to entertain with good will, but you've got to look very carefully to find it. Theseus realizes immediately that Quince isn't "standing" on the right punctuation marks. Lysander sees he doesn't know when to stop. Hippolyta likens him to a child playing on a recorder. But after all, says Theseus, the speech was like a tangled chain: out of order but not broken.

As the characters of the play enter, Quince continues his prologue. He introduces Pyramus, the beauteous Thisby, the vile wall across which the lovers had to speak, and the man in the moon. Introducing the lion, he explains the slight plot. Stealing forth to secretly meet Pyramus by night at Ninus's tomb, Thisby was surprised and scared off by a lion. Her mantle fell as she fled, and the lion bloodied it with his mouth. When Pyramus sees it he thinks Thisby has been killed, and he draws his dagger and kills himself. The rest will be revealed by the play. Notice that Quince works himself up to a lyric pitch by the end. You may feel he has been receiving some coaching from Bottom, whose overwrought, alliterative style is noticeable in the climactic lines: "Whereat, with blade, with bloody blameful blade,/He bravely broached his boiling bloody breast."

NOTE: The "Pyramus and Thisby" plot is very similar, in some respects, to that of Shakespeare's own *Romeo and Juliet*, in which Romeo kills himself after mistakenly thinking that Juliet herself is dead. Shakespeare may have been poking fun at his own work in this parallel, and his audience may even have recognized it. The two plays were probably written around the same time.

Now it is the wall's (Snout's) turn to speak. Try to visualize all of this play within a play as it happens, and you'll be able to appreciate more fully its burlesque comedy. As in a children's play, *seeing* someone dressed up as a wall is a lot more ridiculous than just thinking about it. The wall explains that through a hole or "chink" in it the lovers whispered. Theseus and Demetrius exchange sarcastic comments, though the duke graciously admits that one couldn't expect a wall to speak better.

And here comes the noble Pyramus, with all of Bottom's pent-up theatrical energy. He immediately explodes with a series of exclamations and "O's"; why say something once when you can say it three times, "alack, alack, alack"? Pyramus decries the night and praises the wall, and takes eight lines to say what might have been said in one. The wall holds up his fingers as the chink, but Pyramus peers through to no avail and curses the wall. Imagine Bottom actually looking through Snout's fingers, and you can see some of the problem these actors are going to have in getting their tragicomedy taken seriously.

Theseus says, as an aside, that since the wall is a person, it ought to curse back at Pyramus. He meant it as a joke to his fellow members of the audience, but Bottom has no sense of where the proper parameters of the stage are. He steps out of character and addresses Theseus directly, explaining that the wall shouldn't speak, because the line is actually Thisby's cue to come on stage.

The "lovely" Thisby (Flute) then enters. She speaks to the wall, lamenting how frequently it has kept her and Pyramus apart. How often her cherry lips have kissed its stones, its stones all mixed up with lime and hair. Yecch! Shakespeare never misses a chance to poke fun at his pompous lyricism! The two lovers encounter each other through the hole in the wall, exchanging a trite but confused set of lovers' vows involving the hero Leander (though Bottom mixes up his name with Alexander's) and Helen, and other twisted namings. Their passionate connection reaches its height as they kiss through the chink, though Thisby admits, "I kiss the wall's hole, not your lips at all."

After arranging to meet at "Ninny's" tomb (Bottom has still not gotten the name right), they exit. Having discharged his part (and, one senses, glad to be done with it), the wall also graciously leaves.

Theseus and Demetrius continue joking while again Hippolyta expresses her discomfit with the amateurs. Theseus says that all plays are but shadows, and the worse ones can be made better by the imagination. Theseus suggests his testy wife believe as much in the players as the players do in themselves. That way, they may be seen as excellent men.

NOTE: Again Theseus weaves in his theme of the power of the imagination. Theater is all made up, in a way, of light and shadow. It takes belief and imagination on the part of the audience to make something more substantial. This play within a play and its characters within characters test and challenge our ability to engage our imaginations.

Lines 219–372
Now the lion and the moon enter. The lion delivers just the prologue Bottom •had suggested, revealing himself—so as not to frighten the ladies— to be Snug the joiner. The men in the audience dig in, exchanging jokes about the gentle lion and punning back and forth. When the moon starts to say his part, he is continually interrupted by the heckling of Theseus, Demetrius, Hippolyta, and Lysander. They're having fun at his expense, and you can feel his growing uncomfortableness, at which they only laugh more. He finally finishes his lines, which merely tell who he is and what he represents. When you think of the magical and powerful ways in which the moon and moonlight have been presented in *A Midsummer Night's Dream*,

this moon is absurdly mundane. Again, Shakespeare is poking fun at theatrical conventions. He's already thoroughly bewitched us with his moonshine, so he doesn't have to worry.

Thisby enters, the lion roars, and Thisby flees. Both are commended by the audience. Even the moon draws applause from Hippolyta, who seems finally to have gotten into the spirit of the thing. Now is Pyramus's big moment. With his inflated alliteration ("gracious, golden, glittering gleams"), relentless rhyme scheme, exclamations, and inappropriate terms ("O dainty duck!"), you can recognize Bottom in his high style. And you can also see Shakespeare (an actor himself, remember) mercilessly satirizing a pompous style in Elizabethan theater that he obviously did not think well of. (Critics suggest two kinds of acting were at war in Shakespeare's time. The other, which it is said he preferred, was a more relaxed, natural style.) He calls to the fates to conclude his life. But wait! He's not done yet. Why stop now when you can recite ten more lines? So Bottom curses lions, extols Thisby, calls forth his tears, and draws his sword. Yet more! Bottom won't just do it; he'll tell us he's dying. Finally, at the height of his acting power, he proclaims his own death: "Now am I dead." And proclaims it: "Now die, die, die, die, die."

Again the audience are all over the actors with their joking comments; they don't wait a moment to chime in. When you think about it, Lysander and Demetrius were just recently in a play of their own, acting out their own romantic trials. It's a bit smug of them to be presuming such distance from their complications, now. You, of course, have seen them as players in a plot constructed by Oberon. Their poking fun at the actors reminds us how recently we poked fun at them.

Thisby enters and finds Pyramus dead. She mourns his passing, extolling his "lily lips" and "cherry nose," his "yellow cowslip cheeks," and eyes "green as leeks." Is this a lover's lament or a recipe? Again you can see the ridiculous heights (or depths) to which bad poetry can climb. She calls to the sisters of Fate to end her life since they have already ended Pyramus's. She stabs herself, bidding farewell to her friends, "Adieu, adieu, adieu."

NOTE: Notice how the play "Pyramus and Thisby" mirrors the situation of the lovers in *A Midsummer Night's Dream*. Though the lovers come to happy wedded ends, remember how serious a situation Hermia was in at the beginning of the play. She was threatened with death. This underlying tragic element shows the serious nature of Shakespeare's critique of love. The workingmen's play serves to diffuse this tragic element by virtue of its comedy. It serves almost like an exorcism. Pyramus and Thisby meet their terrible ends amid laughter, not tears. And the lovers, if they can only see it, are presented with a comic rendition of ill-fated, doting love.

Theseus and Demetrius note that the moon, the lion, and the wall are left to bury the dead. This is enough to make Bottom rise from the dead, offering his opinion that the wall has now come down.

He asks if they'd like to see an epilogue to the play, or hear a dance, and you may recognize his typical switching of the words for each action. Theseus pleads for no epilogue. But he agrees that a dance (the country "bergomask") sounds good. And so the company dances.

Theseus announces it's midnight, time for the lovers to go to their beds. He adds, knowing less than we know, that it's almost fairy time, as well. The play, he finds, has done its job of passing the long hours. And can you feel the way in which the performance has relieved the tension for the lovers, giving them a chance to laugh at themselves? Now the newlyweds can retire to their beds, and the celebration of their marriages will continue for two weeks. The duke and duchess and the four lovers, all firmly united in the social and sacred bonds of marriage, leave together. Their world of love has come into its proper order.

Lines 373–440
Now it is moonlight again, and the fairy world returns for a bow, lest—in our sense of social order—we forget the reality of its magical powers. Puck enters with a broom. He describes the scary night world, with its lions roaring and wolves howling, the owl screeching like the dead. This is the time, says Robin, when the graves open and the sprites leap out. But it's also the time of Puck and his fellow fairies. Remember, Oberon previously told us they are "spirits of another sort." Though they too are creatures of the night, they have come to frolic, not to menace. They are here to bless the house of the duke. Puck will even help clean, sweeping out the dust from behind the door.

NOTE: It was popular folklore that Puck helped sweep the house clean at midnight. But notice, as well, how poetically apt his action is. It's as if he were cleaning the *stage* (not just the house) of its illusions, or sweeping the sand from our charmed eyes.

Oberon enters with Titania and all the fairies. He sends light throughout the house and commands his fairies and elves to hop like birds, singing and dancing, bringing cheer. Titania has them all rehearse their song. It's clear that the fairy way of giving blessings is through a magical rite of song and dance. And this lovely gift of grace we get to experience. Oberon sends his sprites through the palace. He and Titania shall bless the bride-bed of Theseus and Hippolyta and assure that their offspring will be happy. All the lovers shall be so blessed: their children will be healthy and well formed, not prey to accidental birth defects. Though again this was a traditional realm attended to by the fairies, Oberon's blessing of natural grace upon the children of the lovers seems to indicate that the natural world has been restored to harmony. Remember the terrible picture he painted when he and Titania were at odds? Now with field-dew he consecrates the house to the ultimate order of peace and harmony. Everyone but Puck leaves the stage.

And Puck, with his usual mischievous gleam, offers us this apology. If you didn't like the play, he says, just pretend that you have "slumb'red here,/ While these visions did appear." In that case, all you have seen is "but a dream." Like Theseus, you can pretend that it was all some airy construction of the imagination. Like the lovers you can cover it over, as if the dream were best forgotten. Or like Bottom you can test it, move toward it, glimpse it, respect its power, and think it over. In the end Shakespeare teases you, pretends innocence, and leaves the serious matter of his comedy for you, the reader or viewer, to judge. Puck admits he is just an actor; theater and spirit magic are the two sides of his face. If he can escape the hisses from his audience, he will play the part the best he can. If you befriend him with your applause, he'll befriend you with his magic.

A STEP BEYOND

Tests and Answers

TESTS

Test 1

1. The three kinds of people Theseus says are ____ under the sway of the imagination are:
   A. the fairies, the lovers, and the workingmen
   B. the lunatic, the lover, and the poet
   C. the audience, the actors, and the playwright

2. The flower's juice that has the ability to make ____ someone fall in love with the next person he or she sees is infused with the power of
   A. Cupid   B. Diana   C. Oberon

3. Titania's favorite resting place is sur- ____ rounded by
   A. birds and bumblebees
   B. fairies   C. flowers

4. Puck's other name is ____
   A. Pyramus   B. Robin Goodfellow
   C. King of Shadows

5. The moon's light is symbolic of ____
   A. the true, clear power of love
   B. the ability of reason to shine through the dark
   C. madness, romance, and magic

6. By having the three weddings take place at ____
   the end of the play, Shakespeare makes us
   feel
   A. that mistaken love and discord have
      come into a harmonious order
   B. that the fairies are not real, and their
      magic is just another way of seeing
      peoples' problems
   C. how ruthless society can be in
      enforcing its laws

7. Bottom's Dream   ____
   A. unlike the lovers', fades as soon as he
      wakes up
   B. shows that the entire play was
      conjured up by him
   C. lingers, holding the mystery of the
      fairy world

8. Athenian law says Hermia must   ____
   A. obey her father's wishes, live as a
      nun, or die
   B. marry the person she was engaged to
      first
   C. do as Theseus tells her

9. "Seeing" is a theme of the play because   ____
   A. those who are charmed have special
      vision
   B. love sees with its own eyes, and
      sometimes love is blind
   C. reality can be seen only with the eyes
      of reason

10. When Oberon and Titania quarrel   _____
    A. it makes all the lovers quarrel too
    B. Bottom is turned into an ass
    C. the natural world is out of order

11. Why are the two sets of young lovers so hard to tell apart?

12. How is the theme of theatrical illusion woven into the play?

13. Describe the importance of flower imagery in the play.

14. How does Theseus's reliance on reason affect his general understanding?

15. What is "doting," and what is its significance in the play?

Test 2

1. Helena calls Hermia a puppet because she   _____
    A. can't make up her mind and is pulled by everyone else's desires
    B. is small
    C. has a funny way of moving when she is angry

2. When Bottom worries about the lion scaring the audience, it   _____
    A. reminds us that theater deals with the dynamics between reality and illusion
    B. is annoying, because he wants to play all the parts
    C. is fascinating because the audience really does show fear during the play

3. Lysander vows eternal love to _____
   A. Hermia B. Helena
   C. both Hermia and Helena

4. Oberon's use of poetic language _____
   A. shows how his flowery speech is
      influenced by flowers
   B. is used by Shakespeare to mock the
      bad poets of his day
   C. shows us his magic; the sounds
      themselves are like a spell

5. Flower symbolism is appropriate to the fairy _____
   world because
   A. the names of flowers sound like magic
      spells
   B. flowers are small miracles of the
      natural world, whose size helps give a
      picture of the fairies' size
   C. reason is behind fairy magic, and
      flowers show the power of scientific
      reasoning

6. When Oberon says the fairies are "spirits _____
   of another sort," he means that
   A. although they are tiny, they are not to
      be trifled with
   B. unlike the lovers, they're possessed of
      true sight
   C. although they are night creatures,
      their intentions are good

7. In the play, activity in the woods is char- _____
   acterized by emotional indulgence and
   magic. Activity in the city is characterized
   by

   A. unruly behavior by boisterous persons
   B. social order and reason
   C. total concentration on commerce

8. It is hard to tell the sets of lovers apart be- _____
cause
   A. they're meant to represent lovers in
      general, not specific characters
   B. they are rarely on stage together
   C. when their eyes are charmed, their
      appearances change also

9. Theseus and Hippolyta represent _____
   A. the power of social institutions,
      marriage, and law
   B. the triumph of Greek over English
      mythology
   C. the blind nature of romantic love

10. The one mortal who really interacts with _____
the fairy world is
   A. Lysander   B. Bottom
   C. Philostrate

11. Compare Bottom's recollection of his magical experiences to that of the lovers.

12. How does Titania's description of the natural world
out of order affect our understanding of the fairies?

13. Why is moonlight so important in the play?

14. Discuss the different ways in which the three groups
of characters speak.

15. How does the content of "Pyramus and Thisby"
reflect on the rest of the play?

ANSWERS

Test 1

1. B   **2.** A   **3.** C   **4.** B   **5.** C   **6.** A
7. C   **8.** A   **9.** B   **10.** C

11. Though Hermia is described as small and dark, and Helena as tall and thin, Lysander and Demetrius are not given physical descriptions at all. They seem to be almost interchangeable. Of course, once the love juice has worked its magic they *are*, in terms of their love, interchangeable. First they both love Hermia; then they both love Helena. By having these lovers so ill-defined, Shakespeare makes them stand for lovers in general, rather than appear as specific characters. All four young people speak the high courtly poetry and romantic clichés of people in love. But love is a power that, like the magic juice, transforms people to its own purposes. In a way they are no longer themselves, but agents of its power—lovers. By keeping his lovers indistinct, Shakespeare shows how love levels people to its own ends, blinding them from seeing the reality of other people in the process.

12. The rustic actors rehearsing their production of "Pyramus and Thisby" give Shakespeare the chance to satirize theatrical conventions and to play with his audience around the limits of the theater's illusion. Bottom worries about how the audience might react to the appearance of a lion or to Pyramus dying. He's afraid they will take these acted roles seriously and not understand that they are in the realm of theater, not "reality." He wants the actors to explain that they are just actors. But theater is based on the audience's ability or willingness to suspend for a time their normal perception of reality and to believe in illusion. Shakespeare tests this suspension to the limit in *A Midsummer Night's Dream* by portraying a mythical, magical world of fairies that is entirely built on illusion. You are asked to believe that this mysterious, fanciful world is real.

13. The fairy world is continually associated with flowers, as well as with other nature-related imagery. This makes flowers part of a world slightly beyond human perception or influence. Flowers and plants have traditionally been associated with magic, and in the case of certain herbs their "magic" curative powers are well proven. And they imbue us with a sense of wonder at their colorful and beautiful forms, in spite of the depth of our scientific knowledge about how they grow. Shakespeare's association of the fairies with these small miracles makes the flowers seem part of an elemental creative power. The fairies are also constantly compared in size to the flowers, giving us an imaginary yardstick by which to measure and to view the fairies (since they are played by human actors on the stage). The conflicting realities of the size we hear about and the size we actually see test our power of imaginative perception.

14. Theseus's reliance on reason removes him, in some degree, from understanding the creative worlds of art and magic. He does not really believe the lovers' story of their magical encounters. His world of war conquests and social order keep him materially grounded. He can only scoff at tales of fairies and magic. We who have already experienced the power and poetry of the fairy world can see that reason, for all its virtue, can also lead to blindness. Theseus compares lovers, madmen, and poets. He says that imagination can lead them all astray. In one way he has a point: we've already seen the ways in which people can be blinded and misled by romantic love. But we've also glimpsed—like Bottom—an unspeakable beauty, a dream vision of flowers, magic, moonlight, and poetic art. A world without these elements might be materially sound, but it lacks a powerful dimension of human experience.

15. "Doting" is used again and again to describe the kind of romance-inspired seeing (and loving) that is essentially blind. In other words, doting is not seeing at all. When Helena is described by Lysander as doting on Demetrius, he means she is so foolishly in love that she can't really judge Demetrius's character; her love stands in the way of her reasonable sight. Similarly, Titania is described by Oberon as doting on Bottom, ass's head and all. Her situation is even clearer. Though we can plainly see the ass before her, her love-transformed eyes see only what they want to see. Ass-headed Bottom is a handsome prince to her. According to Shakespeare, when people dote they are in a dangerous, intoxicated realm, seeing what their mind and heart tell them to see, not what may actually be before them.

Test 2

1. B   **2.** A   **3.** C   **4.** C   **5.** B   **6.** C
7. B   **8.** A   **9.** A   **10.** B

11. The lovers wake up from their dream almost as if they had been knocked out. They have only fuzzy recollections of their strange experiences but are willing to believe that they were just dreaming. Mostly, they seem to want to forget the events and move on toward their now more stable marriages. Bottom, too, wakes up with fuzzy perceptions, but he seems closer to his "dream" experience than do the lovers. It seems almost as if he remembers what happened; his difficulty is in finding a way to talk about it. He approaches the experience and retreats from it, but ultimately holds it in a kind of suspension. Even if he can't fully talk about this "vision," he won't dismiss it. Intuitively, Bottom seeks to keep hold of his dream through the transforming means of art: he immediately decides to write a ballad called "Bottom's Dream" to be performed during the play.

12. Because of the fairies' constant association with flowers and winged insects and because of Shakespeare's emphasis on their diminutive size, we may get the initial impression that these spirits are cute, tiny, dainty, and harmless. Though Oberon shows a human-like jealousy and vengeance, he doesn't cause any intense trouble (except with his use of the love juice). But Titania's description of the disorder in the natural world resulting from her quarrel with Oberon gives us an entirely different sense of their powers. Now the king and queen of fairyland seem like elemental forces. Their emotional life has gigantic force: it can cause tidal waves and terrible storms, disrupting the general calm and order of human life. Because of the terrifying picture Titania paints, filled with disease and death, our conception of the benign fairies is altered into something more respectful. Their magic world has behind it a primary power, and as its representatives, Oberon and Titania are mighty rulers.

13. Except for the beginning and the end, most of the action of the play takes place at night. Oberon makes clear that night is the fairies' time. Theseus, who is aligned with reason, appears during the daylight portions. The fairies, with all the midsummer madness they set in motion, work their magic at night. Moonlight thus symbolizes emotions, as contrasted to reason, and of course is the favored trysting time of lovers. Oberon is referred to by Puck as the king of shadows, and the shadowy night world he presides over is one of mysterious glimpses and strange behavior. Puck and Theseus both refer to the theater as a place of shadows, so the moonlit night also represents the realm of theater, where theatrical illusions take on the appearance of real life. And for human beings, it is much harder to see in the dark. Since so much of the play is concerned with the difficulty lovers have in "seeing," moonlight thus symbolizes the cloudy light of love in which lovers "dote."

14. The lovers tend to speak a courtly poetry, filled with high-sounding vows and mythical allusions. Their formal speech almost always rhymes—especially in the longer speeches—giving the lovers an artificial sound. Their dialogues contain many clever turns of phrases. Yet nothing much individual comes through about any one of them.

The fairies—especially Oberon and Titania—also speak poetically. But their poetry is distinguished by elegance and grace, not by clichés. It is filled with the names of flowers and small animals, linking the fairies to nature. Oberon's descriptions are precise yet lyrical; his language seems often to be a magical charm in itself. In Titania's description of the natural world off balance, she personifies all the elements of the natural world so that they seem to be human.

The workingmen speak in prose, not poetry. This gives them a feeling of earthiness, of being grounded in the daily world. They continually misuse and mispronounce words. Their discomfit with language makes them perfect vehicles for Shakespeare's satire of bad acting.

15. "Pyramus and Thisby," a story about two lovers kept apart by their parents, reveals a frustrated romantic intrigue similar to that of the lovers in *A Midsummer Night's Dream*. Remember, Hermia and Lysander try to flee Athens at the beginning of the play, because her father's wishes stand between them. "Pyramus and Thisby" shows the unfortunate result that can befall young lovers caught up in their passions. Although Hermia is threatened with death, Thisby and Pyramus do actually die in their play. The material is dealt with comically, but the tragedy is there as a cautionary sign. Things work out well for Hermia and Lysander and for Helena and Demetrius, who end their play comfortably married. Through its comic shenanigans, "Pyramus and Thisby" diffuses the tragic element in its story and releases it through laughter.

Term Paper Ideas and other Topics for Writing

Characters

1. What are the two sides to Theseus's reliance on reason?

2. Describe what is unique about Bottom's dream.

3. Discuss the importance of Puck's final monologue.

4. How are we made to feel Oberon and Titania's power?

5. Discuss the limits Shakespeare places on his characterization of the lovers.

Imagery

Discuss the importance of the following images:

1. Flowers

2. Moonlight

3. The woods

4. Discuss the imagery in Titania's speech about the result of her quarrel with Oberon.

Language

1. How are different kinds of language used for the different sets of characters?

2. Discuss Oberon's use of poetry. In what ways is it magical?

3. Describe and analyze the ways in which the workmen misuse language.

Themes

1. How are the lunatic, the lover, and the poet alike?

2. Discuss the importance of "seeing" for the lovers.

3. Discuss the relation between illusion and reality in the theater.

4. Discuss the importance of dreaming in the play.

5. Does Shakespeare intend us to see the fairy world as real? How does he play with our perceptions?

6. Relate Bottom's dream to the interplay between reason and imagination.

7. Love is blind. How does the play show that?

8. Discuss the difference in this play between the city and the woods.

9. How does the idea of marriage function in the play?

Theater

1. In what ways do the settings give meaning to the play?

2. How would you portray the fairy world if you were a director? What would be its properties?

3. In what ways does "Pyramus and Thisby" reflect on the rest of the play and on the nature of theater itself?

4. How do the different realms interrelate and give a sense of structure to the play?

5. How is Oberon a director or playwright?

6. Puck calls Oberon the king of shadows. In what ways might we see Shakespeare as the king of shadows?

The Play

1. Compare and contrast the treatment of love in *A Midsummer Night's Dream* and *Romeo and Juliet*.

2. Compare and contrast the magic spirit worlds of *A Midsummer Night's Dream* and *The Tempest*.

3. How do *A Midsummer Night's Dream* and *Romeo and Juliet* illustrate the difference between comedy and tragedy?

Further Reading

CRITICAL WORKS

Arthos, John. *Shakespeare's Use of Dream and Vision*. Totowa, N.J.: Rowman and Littlefield, 1977.

Chesterton, G. K. *Chesterton on Shakespeare*. Chester Springs, Pa.: Dufour Editions, 1971. Readable essays with a very English sensibility.

Chute, Marchette. *Shakespeare of London*. New York: E. P. Dutton, 1949. A biography that reads like a novel.

Coleridge, S. T. *Shakespearean Criticism*. New York: E. P. Dutton, 1960. A great poet's grasp of Shakespeare's music.

Fender, Stephen. *Shakespeare: A Midsummer Night's Dream*. London: Edward Arnold, 1968.

Garber, Marjorie B. *Dream in Shakespeare*. New Haven and London: Yale University Press, 1974. A penetrating look at Shakespeare's visionary world, including a psychological analysis of dreams.

Granville-Barker, Harley. *More Prefaces to Shakespeare*. Princeton, N.J.: Princeton University Press, 1974. Insightful essays by a great Shakespearean director.

Kermode, Frank. *Shakespeare, Spenser, Donne*. New York:

Viking Press, 1971. An essay that includes the occult philosophical tradition behind Shakespeare's magic.

Lerner, Lawrence, ed. *Shakespeare's Comedies: An Anthology of Modern Criticism*. Baltimore, Md.: Penguin Books, 1978.

Nagler, Alois M. *Shakespeare's Stage*. New Haven: Yale University Press, 1981. The classic introduction to the Elizabethan stage.

Parott, Thomas Marc. *William Shakespeare: A Handbook*. New York: Charles Scribner's Sons, 1955.

Shakespeare, William. *A Midsummer Night's Dream*. Edited by Harold F. Brooks. The Arden Shakespeare. London: Methuen, 1979. Fully annotated, with extensive introductory notes.

Van Doren, Mark. *Shakespeare*. New York: Henry Holt, 1939.

Young, David P. *Something of Great Constancy: The Art of a Midsummer Night's Dream*. New Haven: Yale University Press, 1966.

AUTHOR'S WORKS

Shakespeare wrote 37 plays (38 if you include *The Two Noble Kinsmen*) over a 20-year period, from about 1590 to 1610. It's difficult to determine the exact dates when many were written, but scholars have made the following intelligent guesses about his plays and poems:

Plays

1588–93	*The Comedy of Errors*
1588–94	*Love's Labour's Lost*
1590–91	*2 Henry VI*
1590–91	*3 Henry VI*
1591–92	*1 Henry VI*
1592–93	*Richard III*

1592–94	*Titus Andronicus*
1593–94	*The Taming of the Shrew*
1593–95	*The Two Gentlemen of Verona*
1594–96	*Romeo and Juliet*
1595	*Richard II*
1594–96	*A Midsummer Night's Dream*
1596–97	*King John*
1596–97	*The Merchant of Venice*
1597	*1 Henry IV*
1597–98	*2 Henry IV*
1598–1600	*Much Ado About Nothing*
1598–99	*Henry V*
1599	*Julius Caesar*
1599–1600	*As You Like It*
1599–1600	*Twelfth Night*
1600–01	*Hamlet*
1597–1601	*The Merry Wives of Windsor*
1601–02	*Troilus and Cressida*
1602–04	*All's Well That Ends Well*
1603–04	*Othello*
1604	*Measure for Measure*
1605–06	*King Lear*
1605–06	*Macbeth*
1606–07	*Antony and Cleopatra*
1605–08	*Timon of Athens*
1607–09	*Coriolanus*
1608–09	*Pericles*
1609–10	*Cymbeline*
1610–11	*The Winter's Tale*
1611–12	*The Tempest*
1612–13	*Henry VIII*

Poems

| 1592 | *Venus and Adonis* |
| 1593–94 | *The Rape of Lucrece* |

1593–1600   *Sonnets*
1600–01   *The Phoenix and the Turtle*

The Critics

The Play

"A Midsummer Night's Dream" shines like "Romeo and Juliet" in darkness, but shines merrily. Lysander, one of the two nonentities who are its heroes, complains at the beginning about the brevity of love's course . . . :

So quick bright things come to confusion.

This, however, is at the beginning. Bright things will come to clarity in a playful, sparkling night while fountains gush and spangled starlight betrays the presence in a wood near Athens of magic persons who can girdle the earth in forty minutes and bring any cure for human woe. Nor will the woe to be cured have any power to elicit our anxiety. . . . There will be no pretense that reason and love keep company, or that because they do not death lurks at the horizon.

—*Mark Van Doren*, Shakespeare, 1939

Characterization

In *A Midsummer Night's Dream*, then, Shakespeare defines his characters according to what they represent, according to their labels. The lovers are not individuals, they are "lovers," and the definition of that word will determine their behaviour; Puck's actions too are predicted by the definition of "Puck." Nor is the process restricted to characters; even places stand for something, are labels. Athens, established in literary tradition as the legendary seat of reason (in Boccaccio's *Teseida* and "The Knight's Tale") is here almost a byword for rational order. The wilderness outside Athens is called a "wood" and not a forest, as is the corresponding locale in *As You Like It*, because it must also be a label for "mad," and in case we miss the point, Demetrius is made to pun on "wood" (for "mad" and "forest") and "wooed"; "And here am I, and wood within this wood. . . ." With everything so clearly defined and with the infinite complexities of realistic character and "real life" settings so firmly excised, no wonder those who came looking for realism go away convinced that the play is a little too simple.

—*Stephen Fender*, Shakespeare:
A Midsummer Night's Dream,
1968

The End of the Play

If ever the son of man in his wanderings was at home and drinking by the fireside, he is at home in the house of Theseus. All the dreams have been forgotten, as a melancholy dream remembered throughout the morning might be forgotten in the human certainty of any other triumphant evening party; and so the play seems naturally ended. It began on the earth and it ends on the earth. Thus to round off the whole midsummer night's dream in an eclipse of daylight is an effect of genius. But of this comedy, as I have said, the mark is that genius goes beyond itself; and one touch is added which makes the play colossal. Theseus and his train retire with a crashing finale, full of humour and wisdom and things set right, and silence falls on the house. Then there comes a faint sound of little feet, and for a moment, as it were, the elves look into the house, asking which is the reality. "Suppose we are the realities and they the shadows." If that ending were acted properly any modern man would feel shaken to his marrow if he had to walk home from the theatre through a country lane.

—*G. K. Chesterton*, Chesterton On
Shakespeare, 1971

Shakespeare's Poetic Speeches

No, his heart was in these passages of verse, and so the heart of the play is in them. And the secret of the play—the refutation of all doctrinaire criticism of it—lies in the fact that though they may offend against every letter of dramatic law they fulfil the inmost spirit of it, inasmuch as they are dramatic in themselves. They are instinct with that excitement, that spontaneity, that sense of emotional overflow which is drama. They are as carefully constructed for effective speaking as a messenger's speech in a Greek drama. One passage in particular, Puck's "My mistress with a monster is in love," is both in idea and form, in its tension, climax, and rounding off, a true messenger's speech. Shakespeare, I say, was from the first a playwright in spite of himself. Even when he seems to sacrifice drama to poem he—instinctively or not—manages to make the poem itself more dramatic than the drama he sacrifices.

—*Harley Granville-Barker*, More Prefaces to Shakespeare, 1974

Bottom's "Vision"

By contrast "vision," as it is introduced into the play, is a code word for the dream understood, the dream correctly valued. Often the user does not know that he knows; this is another of the play's thematic patterns, supporting the elevation of the irrational above the merely rational. As a device it is related to a character type always present in Shakespeare, but more highly refined in the later plays, that of the wise fool. Thus Bottom, awakening, is immediately and intuitively impressed with the significance of his "dream," which we of course recognize as not a dream at all, but rather a literal reality within the play.

—*Marjorie B. Garber*, Dream In Shakespeare, 1974

The Fairies

What is true of the moon applies to the fairies. They are a curious mixture of wood spirits and household gods, pagan deities and local pixies. They inhabit the environs of Athens and follow the fortunes of Theseus and Hippolyta, but they are clearly the spirits

whom we can consider "almost essential to a Midsummer Play," detectably English in character and
habit. Through Titania and her train, Shakespeare
emphasizes their innocence and delicacy; in Oberon
and Puck, he expresses their darker side, potentially
malevolent in the lore of the time.

> —*David P. Young*, Something of
> Great Constancy: The Art of A
> Midsummer Night's Dream,
> 1966

The Comedy of Language

The *Dream's* comedy of language attains its peak of
extravagance in "Pyramus." One favourite effect is
continued from the play proper: the misassignment
of sense-experience—Pyramus sees a voice, hopes
to hear his Thisbe's face, and bids his tongue lose
its light. In the rehearsal-scene he is supposed to
have gone "but to see a noise that he heard," and
the effect has been taken to its highest point in Bottom's garbling of St. Paul: "The eye of man hath
not heard. . . ." That parody would not have been
possible in anything but comic prose; and prose, as
is normal in Shakespeare, is the vehicle for the scenes
of plebeian comedy. Bottom's adherence to it in
fairyland, while Titania speaks verse, adds to the
characterization and the comic effect, emphasizing
how unshakeably he remains himself, and how out
of touch, inhabiting still their disparate worlds, they
are with each other.

> —*Harold F. Brooks*, Introduction to
> Arden, A Midsummer Night's
> Dream, 1979

NOTES

NOTES

NOTES

NOTES